Contest

The Aquatic Hall of Fame and Museum of Canada, Pan Am Pool, Winnipeg, Manitoba
Photo by Gilbert Dong

CONTEST

*Essays on
Sports, Culture,
and Politics*

GARY GENOSKO

ARBEITER RING PUBLISHING • WINNIPEG

Arbeiter Ring Publishing
2-91 Albert Street
Winnipeg, Manitoba
Canada R3B 1G5
arbeiter@tao.ca
www.tao.ca/~arbeiter/

Canadian Cataloguing in Publication Data

Genosko, Gary, 1959–

    Contest

      ISBN 1-894037-06-5

1. Sports – Social aspects. 2. Sports – Philosophy.
I. Title

GV706.5.G45 1999 306.4'83   C99-920081-X

The truth is this: *for alarmingly large chunks of an average day, I am a moron.*

– Nick Hornby, *Fever Pitch: A Fan's Life*

Why, you might ask, would a man give up a promising literary career – there were some good notices – to become a sportswriter?

– Richard Ford, *The Sportswriter*

Contents

ACKNOWLEDGEMENTS

The idea

of writing a sports column directed at a non-sports, that is, arts and politics audience occurred to me about four years ago. Since that time I have written such a column for *Borderlines* magazine. I am grateful for the encouragement of Stan Fogel, Julie Jenkinson and Julia Creet. Over the course of the last four years I discovered many closeted sports fans among my academic and radical colleagues, and they discovered my secret passions. I wrote a lot, perhaps too much, about hockey; I rediscovered my love of swimming; I have never forgotten the cruel beauty and cultural and political power of boxing. I inflated the most banal events with abstruse theoretical concepts, and found sporting tidbits in the most Byzantine theory texts. I read Don DeLillo as a sportswriter. I began watching television again as a form of research! I got carried away about these topics in London and Melbourne, not to mention in Toronto and Winnipeg. I even played a bit.

The *Borderlines* columns have ended. But I found myself with the basis for a book. Together with a few other sports-related articles that I had published over the years in such diverse places as *Fuse* art magazine, *can* book and culture review, the *Kingston Whig-Standard*, and the *International Journal of Psycho-Analysis*, I created a working draft. A good deal of new material came along as a result of visits to the Pan Am Pool in Winnipeg, a place of ineluctable sadness, and by browsing through the wonderfully obscure collection of used sports books at This Ain't the Rosedale Library in Toronto. Daniel Gawthrop kindly brought me up-to-date on his activities at a crucial moment. I am grateful for Craig Morrison's assistance in the collection of material about skateboard culture; likewise, special thanks is due to Timothy Dylan Wood for his research efforts. John and Todd at Arbeiter Ring kept me on my toes and fed me books and urls. Special thanks to Cathy Kuryk for the cover image, and to Gilbert Dong for the frontispiece photo.

I am grateful that my wonderful daughter Hannah will watch a few minutes of hockey with me every Saturday during a season that has become interminable.

The German-Jewish

philosopher and social critic, Max Horkheimer, once quipped that far from having led to its downfall, toothpaste had *become* metaphysics. Even more than oral hygiene products, if any single commodity has come to replace traditional metaphysics in late capitalism – or at least merge with it in often unpredictable and bizarre ways – it is sports.

While writers have taken a wide range of sports as opportunities for philosophical speculation – W.P. Kinsella, Joyce Carol Oates, Eduardo Galeano, Nick Hornby – these writings remain for the most part at the level of fiction, essay, and autobiography. Apart from the odd mass psychologist or behaviourist, few have attempted to engage the cultural, social and political dynamics of sports. In particular, few attempts have been made to unravel the complex relationship between sports and identity in an interesting, readable and provocative way. Gary Genosko breaks significant new ground in this direction

As new social subjects gain entry into those forms of sports culture from which they had until now been excluded, it becomes increasingly evident how sports isn't simply an innocent and banal part of life: sports as mere entertainment. It is, rather, as much a field of power as it is a field of dreams. From time to time, this becomes clear: Jesse Owens in Munich; Jackie Robinson's appearance with the Brooklyn Dodgers as the first black player in major league baseball; Cassius Clay's transformation into Muhammad Ali and, of course, the unforgettable "Black Power" salutes of John Carlos and Tommie Smith at the 1968 Olympics in Mexico

City. While such instances raise the question of the relationship between sports and power, they have generally been perceived as external to the sports themselves.

In Britain, however, there was no denying that sports was the place where questions of identity were broached in an explicit way. It is no coincidence, therefore, that Britain's pre-eminent sociologist, Anthony Giddens, an authority on reflexive social theory, the nature of modern society and identity, initially cut his teeth on the sociology of sport. In Britain, unlike Canada and the US, social contradictions were less easily disguised through an egalitarian rhetoric of the New World, and the pretense that class didn't exist was simply not a possibility. That you were a centre forward rather than a fast-bowler not only indicated your place on the pitch, but also your place within a rigidly structured social order as a whole. It is significant, for instance, that cricket, the sport of the bourgeoisie, came to be disseminated throughout the Empire, to the West Indies, South Africa, India, Pakistan and Australia (though interestingly, not Canada), while the more proletarian sport of football was accorded a much more chequered reception. Once taken up in the periphery, however, the social meanings attached to cricket were irreversibly transformed.

The experience of finding themselves in a football stadium as a part of an undifferentiated mass of supporters adorned with identical colours and symbols, singing the same songs, and employing identical gestures, provided individuals with an intense, often intoxicating, sense of self at the very moment, paradoxically, that that sense was destroyed. The highly ritualized nature of football served to define the identity of a particular club and its supporters against all others. The distinction between friend and foe that many political thinkers consider to be the very definition of the "political" is intrinsic to the culture of football. As a fan or "supporter," you don't simply want to win the game but, rather, to defeat the enemy; thus, you stand ready to fight to the death for your club. Participating in the culture of football, either as a player or a supporter (or both), defines not only your loyalties to a city but also your gender, race, sexual orientation and, most importantly, national identity. The fiercest rivalries in Britain are ultimately not between club teams, but between the national teams of England and Scotland. The nation is articulated through the distinction between those who participate in a specific football culture and those who do not. It is for this reason that fascist parties such as the National Front and the British Movement have historically chosen the football stadium as their happy hunting grounds for new recruits.

Since the 1970s, black players have been grudgingly accepted within the sport, through

12

the pioneering efforts of Cyrille Regis and Viv Anderson. Yet black supporters have only been comparatively recent arrivals in the football world. Asians for the most part remain excluded. Despite the celebrations of the new, modern Britain – "Cool Britannia" – associated with the Labour Party, football remains the last redoubt of hegemonic articulations of identity and difference. I recall a particularly harrowing yet deeply ironic journey from Aberdeen, Scotland to London with a bunch of drunken Arsenal supporters who gleefully targeted me as the only "Paki" on the train. I doubt that, had I made mention of the fact that I had been in Aberdeen for a "trial" or tryout with the Scottish Premier League club (which was the case), it would have made any difference. That is, even if they had believed me. I suspect that not much has changed in the ensuing decade and a half.

The violence with which the particular configurations of identity within football is defended can be readily discerned in the case of Justin Fashanu. Fashanu, the son of a Nigerian barrister born in Shoreditch, London, made his debut with Norwich City at age eighteen in 1979. Shortly thereafter he went on to become the first million pound black player upon being transferred to Nottingham Forest where he stayed for the next couple of years. He was eventually bounced out of the Premier League after a volatile career with a host of British clubs then on to Canada and eventually the US. The reason Fashanu fell from grace was that, while his sexual preferences had been common knowledge within football, in 1990 he "came out" and bravely declared to the world that he was gay. In a highly conformist sport, Fashanu dared to express his individuality. While white supporters could bring themselves to identify with the supposed strength and virility of the heterosexual, black male body, the prospect of a queer black player was well beyond the pale, so to speak. It was far too great a threat to working class masculinity. All of this spelled disaster for Fashanu and his career. He was given the cold shoulder by his former teammates while his manager at Forest, Brian Clough, described him as "a bloody poof." Perhaps most tragic, his own brother, John, also a high profile player, disowned him as well. Sadly, Fashanu died under mysterious circumstances in Shoreditch last spring amidst a sexual scandal.

If football is a mode through which national identity is often violently constituted and reconstituted, then hockey plays a similarly irreducible role in the formation of Canadian identity. Roch Carrier's celebrated short story, "The Hockey Sweater," which centres on the fierce rivalry between the Leafs and the Habs, goes further towards expressing the complexities of the "two solitudes" than any dry scholarly account of Canadian identity ever could. The

13

single most important historical event in this country after the British North America Act of 1867 was not the two world wars nor the October Crisis, but rather the Canada Cup Series of 1972. It was at this time – and perhaps only during this fabled series – that Canadians came close to imagining themselves as part of a single national community. Canadian identity, as with other forms of cultural belonging, was predicated on a remembrance of things past; on the ability to recall exactly where you were when Paul Henderson scored the winning goal of the game and of the historic series.

The definitive role of hockey in crystallizing a certain kind of "imagined community" only becomes apparent, paradoxically, once cracks appear in the edifice of the specific community that it imagines. The increasing participation of blacks who, as Genosko shows so well, were present as "invisible men" all along, in addition to the growing numbers of women and girls playing the sport, places the cultural politics of hockey squarely within the public domain. The importance of hockey in maintaining a particular, sexualized national identity is rather starkly reiterated every time Don Cherry, flamboyant CBC *Hockey Night in Canada* commentator, makes derisory remarks about the apparent effeminacy of European players, contrasting it with the toughness of "our boys." Such remarks have a profound resonance beyond hockey itself and are the flip-side of Elvis Stojko's recent declaration that his style and technique were misunderstood because he was a "masculine figure skater."

In Britain, football has a profound impact upon alternative culture. For instance, both the *New Musical Express* and *Melody Maker*, the most prominent fixtures of the alternative music press, are littered with references to the sport. Many of the bands they cover employ subtle references to their favourite clubs as a way of subverting or "detourning" dominant cultural formations. In North America, the emergence of a "hip hop nation" has brought to the fore the close relationship between music and certain teams like the Chicago Bulls and the Oakland Raiders. The same cannot be said of the various "alternative" scenes. With the odd exception – for instance, the video for D.O.A.'s cover of B.T.O.'s "Taking Care of Business," shows the Vancouver punk band sticking it to a team of investment bankers on the ice – the North American alternative music scene has been largely indifferent to established sports. It has, however, embraced newer or emergent "extreme" sports which are woven into networks of alternative culture; skateboarding, for example, emerged as an intrinsic part of the West Coast punk scene in the early 1980s.

Skateboarding seeks to rethink the possibilities of the city's built environment; to reimagine ways in which urban spaces can be experienced, transformed and remembered. Skating aggressively, often dangerously, through deserted financial precincts of urban centres after dark, enables people to reclaim these spaces and invest them with radically different meanings; meanings that directly contest those ascribed to them by the corporate culture that rules during the day. Skating is as much about politics, music, and even art, as it is about sports.

Genosko is perhaps best read as a skateboarder. Like the skater, he works (and plays) surreptitiously, after night falls on the city. Refusing to be constrained by "normal" uses of the space, he deterritorializes or undermines traditional, metaphysical notions of "ground," "edifice," "base" and "superstructure." Genosko practices what he calls "un-disciplined theory," which is not to say, however, that he is lazy. To the contrary. But what exactly is it to be undisciplined? For Genosko, it is to adopt a practice of reading and writing unrelentingly against the grain; it is, as he puts it himself, "to read theory as a sports writer, or write sports as a theorist." By reading theory through sports and sports through theory, Genosko persists in occupying the social spaces (and places) of each, yet differently. Who but an undisciplined theorist could uncover the subtle ways in which sporting cultures work to discipline particular identities? Who could push to extremes, deconstruct and ultimately reinvest these cultures with radically different meanings even at the salutary risk of occasionally destroying meaning itself?

As skateboarders will readily attest, though, to be undisciplined is to risk pissing everybody off. Not that this is such a bad thing. Canadian intellectuals are too often reluctant to assume the risk. Like extreme skating, undisciplined theory requires energy, determination and, above all, guts.

– Samir Gandesha
Toronto, Winter, 1999

Why is

the Aquatic Hall of Fame and Museum of Canada on the prairie? On the prairie, water is always an event, even if it is confined to an indoor pool such as the Pan Am Pool in Winnipeg. Despite this museum's proximity to water it is imbued with the dryness of the air and openness of the sky. It occupies the impressive box-like rotunda of the Pan Am complex originally constructed for the 1967 games. Three stories of light pour through the west-facing wall of glass, illuminating the boarded-up ticket booths; the jogging track runs through the space like a river that refuses to be redirected. Around and around the joggers go along the hallways that constitute the museum's wings, and into the heat of the big box for an educated sweat. They are the museum's only regular customers, but whether they notice anything in the collection is unclear. Dust, heat, openness, and an incredibly tall ceiling: this is a museum of the prairie to be sure.

The Aquatic Hall of Fame suffers from neglect, like the Pan Am Pool itself for, despite recent renovations in anticipation of the arrival of the same second division sporting event thirty years after the fact (the Pan Am Games revisited), the pool's administration is stuck in the 1960s: no computers, a dusty Hall of Fame, an unused terrace before the rotunda, snack bars unintentionally rich in collectible bric-a-brac, and a tangible sadness in the air which comes with the abandonment of a public resource. Not even the stench of chlorine can smother the whiff of Tory scandal.

The museum has been left to fend for itself. The visitor is left with the unmistakable impression that the heroic efforts of Vaughn Baird, the local lawyer to whose energy and influence in international athletics the museum owes so much, have been relegated to a glorious past; a past, incidentally, that is quite recent. Today, a sole volunteer is in charge of the museum. It would be unfair to say that the only task remaining for the museum is to catalogue its own inexorable slide into desuetude; yet, the visitor is driven toward this conclusion.

There are signs of life here and there, but they are largely buried in poorly documented events, fading pamphlets and posters, forgotten names, and anonymous bits and pieces of the eclectic collection. Consider, for instance, the "stolen" banner from the Munich Olympics of 1972, a massive eight-by-four-foot orange flag, framed and mounted, along with the requisite newspaper clippings detailing the scandal of the delivery of the flag to Baird and the protests of the German National Olympic Committee. But this "flag of war" has been bleached by the prairie sun that pours through the disused entrance way in which it is mounted.

The Greek and Roman gods Poseiden and Neptune are much in evidence. The rotunda has two massive twenty-foot high aluminium and glass hangings by Suzanne Hare evoking Poseiden's "Poetry" and "Tears." On ground level below these dusty abstract hangings are more traditional bronzes, suitable for unveiling by politicians, the names of whom, such as Jean Charest, are mythically ennobled by the ancient gods of the sea; Charest is still presented as a saviour of sorts.

In the same display cases one can find bronze buffaloes, turtles from the shops of taxidermists, glass fish, porcelain bowls, stone birds, and many other undocumented pieces. The collection is heavy with kitsch: commemorative plates abound – Dali, Churchill, Queen Elizabeth – as do fossilized fish, model boats, diver's helmets, nautical gear, no end of Greek, Mexican, and Aboriginal artifacts; sponges, sea shells, bison statuettes, comic sailors and pirates, this and that, nets – everything, in short, has been thrown into this pool. The display cases are profoundly free associative and the juxtapositions surely surrealistic, despite themselves. This curatorial wantonness and indiscretion knows no bounds: the cases displaying this stuff are regularly sprayed with the salt smells of the sea by the sweat of joggers passing by them. Sweaty joggers roll along like the tides and this unorchestrated effect brings the collection to life, while imperilling the inattentive visitor; thank god there are few of these.

Andre Durand's massive paintings are mounted high in the rotunda. His huge painting of Sasha Baumann, as well as his equally massive "Olympiad Symposium," are masterfully heroic and homoerotic testaments to the "paradoxical masculinity," to borrow Brian Pronger's term, of the great Canadian swimmer; that is, masculinity is embraced and celebrated in neoclassical motifs of vintage postmodernism and simultaneously transgressed through its homoeroticization. Durand's work is far removed, in both time and place, from the athletic male nudes of British painter Duncan Grant (especially *Bathing* [1911] and the much later *Basketball Game* [1960]) to which Pronger points as examples "classic aesthetic homoeroticism." Durand's paintings lie somewhere between the manifest eroticization of young male athletic bodies evident in the work of Grant and the notorious beefcake photo of the late Canadian swimmer Victor Davis, on display in the west hall of the museum. Davis' poster for Speedo bathing suits, for which he posed after he set the world record for the breast stroke at the L.A. Olympics, "made its way into the homes of numbers of gay men."[1] Pronger explains that Speedo denied him permission to reproduce this poster in his study of sports and homosexuality and the company was, as far as public statements are concerned, unaware of its strong homoerotic appeal. Today, of course, cultural theorists would make a great deal out of the creative, perhaps even subversive, decoding practices that turned the Davis poster into a homoerotic masterpiece, displacing it from the heavily travelled zone of heterosexual desire communicated by the poster boy and pin-up. When another celebrated Canadian swimmer, Mark Tewksbury, officially came out this past year, his press conference had the staleness of yesterday's news for the gay community in Toronto. Nonetheless, despite the personal importance of an event of this nature and its integration into the public narrative of the coming-out confession, it is still difficult to absorb into typical sports narratives, and this gives it a singular flavour which isn't exchangeable for the classic tensions of races in the pool, the nationalistic pursuit of gold, and the sponsorships of the victor.

In the museum, however, these effects are muted if only because of the jumble of competing images: images of Davis, Baumann, and Tewksbury, together with their medals, exist alongside photographs of sharks, fantasy art depicting chunky male nudes cavorting with dolphins, portraits of Elizabeth and Philip, David Hockney posters, etc. The clutter itself, rather than those things that break through it, is fascinating. The important pieces wallow with the rest in a great democracy of things.

The west hall is devoted to inductees but contains everything from baptismal waters from the Pacific, Atlantic, and Arctic Oceans which were contributed to the Pan Am Pool in 1967, as well as other, more local extractions from the Red and Assiniboine rivers, not to forget a splash from the International Swimming Hall of Fame in Fort Lauderdale, vintage 1974. All along the hallway one may read the names of great swimmers – racers, divers, synchronized – and wonder at their suits. Other than medals, newspaper clippings and the odd poster carrying the big names and events, what else is there that a swimmer can contribute to the museum but his or her suit? Dry, flat, folded, and mounted behind glass, these suits are antidotes to fetish objects: in their present state they lack a real connection with the bodies of the persons who once wore them. They cannot be easily substituted for the sexual object of interest. Even the sequined suits and elaborate headgear of synchronized swimmers have a freeze-dried appearance, and this is the great irony of a swimming hall of fame. These swimsuits are quite separate from the bodies that wore them, confounding coprophilic pleasure in smelling and the visual scopophilic instinct alike. Ultimately, perhaps, this is pathological, much more so than fetishism.

20   The east hall is rich in tourist kitsch retrieved by athletes from their trips to various events. Official gear – Olympic, Commonwealth, World Aquatic games – is carefully laundered and folded: dozens of t-shirts and team jackets, sweatsuits, ties – a veritable locker room full of sports wear is on display in a model lost and found. Dozens of covers of *Swim* magazine grace one poorly lit wall space; local minor celebrities are feted such as Russ Saunders, model for Dali's *Christ de Saint Jean de la Croix*, and former Canadian Diving Champion and Hollywood stuntman. Princess Di shares space with Buster Crabbe and Johnny Weissmuller.

One can only marvel at this fantastic flea market of Canadian swimming culture. It is disorderly and lacks focus; its internal boundaries are fluid; its exhibits – a professional term whose pretentiousness is fully revealed in this context – tend to drift and embrace ambiguity. The museum is at once a showcase of homoerotic athleticism and a textbook example of studious asexualism in the service of a higher, more noble calling called athletic competition and its selfless administration. The museum issues a challenge to reviewers and eager hermeneuts desperately seeking meaning and clean lines of interpretation. The museum's hallways are long; nooks and crannies abound in the form of disused exits, staircases with a few randomly scattered posters and memorabilia, and shadowy vomitoria leading from the vacant viewing gallery. It would be ridiculous to make this museum speak its truth for it is fundamentally inarticulate. And therein lies its charm.

Notes

1. Brian Pronger, *The Arena of Masculinity: Sports, Homosexuality, and the Meaning of Sex*, Toronto: University of Toronto Press, 1990, p. 191.

WHAT DO YOU WANT FROM LIFE? A KIDNEY-SHAPED POOL

There is

an indescribable something that is at once horrifying and inviting about an aerial shot of Californian suburbs with their kidney-shaped blobs of blue. Although numerous rectangular and other shapes are also in evidence, these surely are the diseased organs of a suburban garden against which putatively healthier organs must be measured; or, perhaps it's the other way around, which suggests that the kidney-shape is like a mutating cell stained blue for the purposes of microscopic investigation. In such an unnatural environment, critical distinctions such as these are hard to make and even harder to maintain.

Kidney bean- and boomerang-shaped figures were emblematic of 1940s and 50s design. They were not confined to swimming pools, of course. But the kidney-shaped pool is a cliché worthy of investigation. Regardless of whether the shape is embedded in a survey of biomorphic design and sculpture of the period, or in the history of residential swimming pool design, the figure of the bean or organ calls attention to itself for its remarkable popularity and longevity. "What do you want from life?" sang Fee Waybill of The Tubes, a long-forgotten late glam, proto-punk band, to which he answered: "A kidney-shaped pool."

Who invented the kidney-shaped pool? While the search for origins is rarely definitive and often illusory, most look to landscape architect Thomas Church (1902-78). Church's historic Donnell pool in Sonoma, California was built in 1948 on the Donnell ranch. Church's design was later adapted for the mass-produced pools that found a market in the 1960s. The Donnell pool still survives today and is featured in most contemporary studies of pool design. Before it gained widespread popularity, Church's design, which included an Arpesque water sculpture, was a model of simplicity which extended beyond the water onto the stone of the deck, the trees on the shaded side of the yard, and the low plantings. Compared with Church's other famous pool, the Hillsborough pool of 1959, with its raised terraces and architectural sculptures, waterfall, and the absence of a diving board and railed access steps, the Donnell pool eschewed sober rectangularity and straight lines for the convex and concave sides of a form adequate to the movement of the water it gracefully nestles.

The mass production of the kidney-shaped pool is equivalent to the mutation of a diseased cell. This is the cultural metastasis of our time and it warrants our critical attention.

IS THAT A HOCKEY PLAYER AT THE BOTTOM OF THE POOL?

Hockey players

lament the coming of spring and the slow meltdown of outdoor rinks. Swimmers rejoice at the return of warm air in early summer as the time nears to fill outdoor pools. Now hockey players and swimmers can indulge in mutually satisfying pastimes by joining an underwater hockey league.

Underwater hockey is played at the bottom of swimming pools, preferably outdoor venues. Each player needs a mask, snorkel, flippers, a protective mitt, and a special stick. No oxygen tanks are allowed. The game is played with a lead puck encased in plastic; an Australian pink puck was used at the recent 1998 World Underwater Hockey Championships in San Jose at the San Jose University Aquatic Center. The teams play six a side and substitutions may be made during play and after stoppages, which occur after goals, penalty calls, and the end of periods. The game is divided into two periods of some fifteen minutes each. The teams change ends at halftime. For the championship, drug testing is in effect according to IOC standards.

The game is catching on in the US. It began as a college craze, but more teams are popping up all around the country beyond the ivory towers; the international presence is impressive, as anyone may see from visiting The Underwater Hockey Tourist and UWH Web sites at *www.getwild.com/sports/122r/going_2_extremes/index.html* and *www.geocities.com/Colosseum/Arena/6300/uwhcinfo1.html*.

SWIMMING WITH THE BULLS

All sorts

of things can be found in swimming pools. A fair number of rock stars have been found floating face down in them; occasionally, a car will end up in one; televisions, lawn furniture, clothing, bottles, all sorts of insects, and screeching cats have all found their way, in one manner or another, into pools.

America may be ready for underwater hockey, but is it ready for *taureaux piscine*? Who would put a bull in a pool? In his contribution to *Splash! Great Writing About Swimming*, edited by Laurel Blossom, Calvin Trillin sets the scene:

> The arena looked like the bullfight arena of a Spanish provincial town except, of course, that in the middle of the ring there was a swimming pool – a rather small swimming pool, with only a couple of feet of water in it, but still a swimming pool. From the stands it looked like one of those plastic swimming pools that people in the suburbs buy at the discount store and stick out in the back yard for the smaller kids to splash around in. There were a few dozen teenage boys in the ring. There was also a bull – a small bull, with blunts on the points of his horns, but still a bull. In other words, the bull in *taureaux piscine* was a bull, and the swimming pool was a swimming pool. Upon my oath.[1]

What was the goal of the match? Simply, to be in the pool at the same time as the bull. It was no easy matter to lure the bull into the pool. The strategies were not elaborate; in a way, they were akin to clowning at a rodeo, except that you had to get into the water with the bull rather than get away from it.

Where else but in France would such a surreal sport pretend to exist? This was a sport of the south, not the south of tourism and film festivals, but the poor south, west of the Rhône towards the Spanish border, and especially around the swamp, the Camargue, with its bull ranches, flamingos, and cowboy culture. And there were other, even wilder variations on the French bullfight, which is on the whole much less graphically violent than the Spanish version: *taureaux football*, for instance, in which two teams play a game of soccer with a bull on the pitch; and *taureaux pastèque*, the goal of which is for the contestants to eat a piece of watermelon in the shortest time possible while sitting on a bench situated in an enclosure in which there is also a bull.

Of course, you say, this is imaginary, this is surrealism. But wait. During the late 1950s a wily bullfight impresario by the name of Emile Bilhau decided, according to Trillin, to "build the gate" by providing entertaining diversions during the regular course of taurine events. So, *taureaux piscine* was the French equivalent of Bat Day at the ballpark, or Ladies Night, or some such thing. And the sport was born.

Trillin's greatest debt, it seems to me, is to Georges Bataille. For Bataille was also inspired by the bullfight, and crafted his splendid pornographic tale, *The Story of the Eye*,[2] around several soft and delicate globular substances – eyes, eggs, testicles – which swirled in a dervish of desire around a historical event, the death of a great matador. But if in Bataille's story all of the cracks, splits and tears in the fabric of the everyday opened onto another world, then in Trillin's story the vehicle that transports us elsewhere is surely the pool. For a bull in the pool changes everything. To say of someone that she or he "swims with the bulls" is a great compliment and comment on that person's bravery and resolve under conditions best described as, well, imaginary.

Notes

1. Calvin Trillin, "Damp in the Afternoon," in *Splash! Great Writing About Swimming*, Laurel Blossom (ed.), Hopewell, N.J.: The Ecco Press, 1996, pp. 229-30.

2. Georges Bataille, *The Story of the Eye*, Joachim Neugroschel (trans.), San Francisco: City Lights Books, 1987.

PICTURES OF LILY

It was

with barely containable glee that Neil Campbell, sports editor at the *Globe & Mail*, announced
in January 1998 that the section would be purchasing and running articles from forthcoming
issues of *Sports Illustrated* magazine. All the usual reasons for buying abroad were trotted out;
the reasons have been, after all, well-rehearsed by private broadcasters in other media. Two
things were, however, different this time around: the capitulation to the status quo constituted a poignant reminder of what progressive voices warned about the effects of split-run
productions of magazines such as *SI*; that is, the growing influence over Canadian magazine
and newspaper publishing of imported material thinly disguised, largely by advertising, as
Canadian, and the slow asphyxiation of Canadian magazines at all levels, especially at the
editorial. On the advertising front, however, the *Globe* was at once buying content from *SI*
and running ads promoting Canadian magazines among which split-run editions do not
count as the real thing. There is no contradiction that can stop the generation of revenue
through advertising in its tracks.

Besides producing redundancy on the newsstands – a cynical manoeuvre, after all, when
there is no longer any point veiling the similarity of products in a line hitherto differentiated
by the frailest of signifiers – the partnership between the *Globe* and *SI* substitutes conven-
ience for relevance. Other closed feedback loops between the *Globe* and Chapters bookstores,

for example, function much the same way by dedifferentiating the book business at all levels. We can all read the same books, in the same atmosphere, drinking the same coffee, and read clever commentary about ourselves wherever there is a *Globe* and Chapters, or a ChaptersGlobe.com.

Every year many of the stories considered to be the best examples of sports writing are taken from *SI*. But this is not what Campbell was so enthusiastic about. The examples from *SI* published by the *Globe* to date overwhelmingly indicate that the magazine is being used as a luxurious wire service with which to cover American football. Such so-called editorial decisions are not based on quality; rather, they are driven by events within the tired range of men's elite sports and the putative need to have them covered, with an editorial attitude not only of acceptance mixed with glee but, surely, of masculine privilege, about the manner in which they are presented.

Campbell also noted that the partnership between the *Globe* and *SI* would not include material from the latter's infamous swimsuit issue, despite the facts that the *Globe* has gone colour, and a recent advertising campaign demonstrated that it likes images of women, preferably undressed. Apparently, some of the male wags in the sports department at the *Globe* were clamouring for the best possible deal. What interests me about Campbell's mention of the swimsuit issue is that its presence is common enough knowledge to support jokes about it; its reputation is such that it can be traded around and commented upon. Any mention of *SI* drags the swimsuit issue in its wake. Of course, by mentioning the swimsuit issue Campbell also deflected attention from the serious matters of the effects of the *Globe*'s growing list of partnerships, the corporatization of Canadian culture, banalization of the book trade, and the fate of Canadian magazines.

Laurel R. Davis' *The Swimsuit Issue and Sport: Hegemonic Masculinity in Sports Illustrated*[1] goes some way in explaining why it is appropriate for Campbell to joke about the swimsuit issue: it is entirely in keeping with the magazine's construction of its ideal reader as a white, heterosexual male who not only enjoys his gender and economic privileges, but consumes the issue as a pleasing diversion from the serious work of sport consumption. Having learned from the feedback that the producers of the swimsuit issue print in the Letters to the Editor section that it is a good thing to define and confirm one's masculinity through leisure, especially the consumption of sexual representations of women, men may deploy a playful attitude to deflect objections as "too critical" and "prudish."

Davis' work towards uncovering and analyzing the ideal reader of the swimsuit issue is rather easy for its encoding is, as she readily admits against certain tendencies in cultural studies to grant to consumers unlimited creative interpretive powers, rather overdetermining, transparent, and influential. At one point she remarks: "I was surprised to find consensus among consumers regarding the basic content and ideal readers of the issue." Indeed, somewhat alarmed at this consensus around the decoding of a fairly obvious content and disabused of unkept theoretical promises, Davis abandons all hope of finding resistant readings to the denotative content of the issue in the mythically produced discursive figure of a hyper- or under-active audience and, instead, gets down to the sociological business of cataloguing its predictable features on the basis of a tiny sample of producers and consumers of the issue. Unfortunately, there is no antidote for this sort of sociology. Still, there is hope for agitation at the connotative level since institutional and textual structuration cannot, after all, solely determine the valuation of public displays of sexuality. This is where things get somewhat more interesting.

There is, on the one hand, an enormously profitable yearly issue falling between the end of football and the beginning of baseball – a ludicrous excuse about dead time that some producers still use to justify the existence and timing of the swimsuit issue – filled with photographs of ideally beautiful women wearing swimsuits (the latter textiles are of secondary interest, related more to the history of *SI*'s coverage of sportswear); the women display all the signs of femininity that reinforce sexism, and this is the content that the ideal readers consume and, in so doing, enhance their masculinity and reinforce the gender (dis)order. By "hegemonic" Davis means "normative," which she diagnoses as colonialist, sexist, heterosexist, racist, and ethnocentric. No mention is made of Antonio Gramsci (perhaps she doesn't know who he is since Gramsci has been slowly erased from the secondary literature in media and cultural studies as the concept of hegemony assumes a more natural, ahistorical profile consonant with the watering down of social and political theory in the social sciences) and Davis shows no interest in the concept's rich history. Clearly, though, *SI*, as well as other magazines, is one of those hegemonic apparatuses by means of which consent to the features of masculinity is manufactured and consolidated.

The women in the swimsuit issue are infantilized, animalized, pose autoerotically, and

29

provide come-on expressions typical of pornography; yet the swimsuit issue is more akin to pin-up material than pornography because of the intersection of the multiple thematics of travel, athleticism, and fashion. While Davis does not delve into the social history of the pin-up, she notes that the swimsuit issue provides (especially in the form of its spin-offs such as calendars) a public badge of masculinity for those men who consume and display it, and serves as a sign vehicle of virility for couch potatoes. More importantly, it shapes the representational needs of boys as they pass into heterosexual adulthood and replaces pin-ups of male athletes with women in swimsuits. Consumed alone or in groups, the swimsuit issue responds to the hormonally driven rally cry of No Masturbation Without Representation with "Pictures of Lily," that old nugget by The Who, constituting a bond between father and son around onanism.

The swimsuit issue is a multiple bridge, then, between boyhood and male adulthood, and football and baseball seasons. It is a device by means of which the producers of *SI* may blend the categories of sport and men's magazines and articulate and refine the magazine's audience in order to deliver them to advertisers. The ability to deliver this relatively affluent group to advertisers (90.9 percent of subscribers are male with a median household income of $51, 389) and reach an extraordinary 21 percent of the men with incomes greater than $25, 000 in the US makes *SI* by far the richest sports magazine, and one of the richest magazines, in terms of advertising revenue, in the country. While not all readers of *SI* appreciate that a sales gimmick like the swimsuit issue has become an institution, it "simply is not a profitable strategy," Davis concludes, for the magazine to heed feminist calls for change in the swimsuit issue and equitable representations of men's and women's sports the remainder of the year. Similarly, the *Globe*'s partnership with Chapters means that henceforth all book reviews are in the service of retail, rather than critical choice, which makes it meaningless to write book reviews for the *Globe*.

The critical issue is whether or not feminist challenges to the gender (dis)order that *SI* reinforces, and through which its readers may conform at least symbolically by cashing in on the cultural capital of the swimsuit issue, can bear the weight of the sorts of claims that Davis wants to make about, for instance, the issue's concealment and delegitimation of the lives of gays and lesbians, since through the construction of its ideal reader *SI* apparently discourages their consumption of the magazine. Davis is not willing to apply her insights into and conclusions about the careful construction of an audience that *SI* very profitably delivers to its advertisers, that is, the economic structure of *SI*, to her social and political demands which remain strangely untouched by this logic. She has no general interest in the relationship between capitalism and desire that would focus her social demands. Indeed, when she does note specific protests against the swimsuit issue and the difficulties they encounter (for example, Linnea Smith's sale of a readymade "protest package" directed against swimsuit issue advertisers), Davis invokes a rather obscure "cause of justice" to buffet her idea of what *SI* should and could be like. Her criticisms are not radical in the sense that they do not have the goal of changing the structure of the media production process. She wants and asks for a little respect but knows perfectly well that it doesn't pay to be respectful.

Despite the banality of Davis' empirical research, its theoretical naïveté and facile identity politicking, her book may be profitably read alongside other recent studies of American magazines such as Christine Lutz and Jane Collins' *Reading National Geographic,*[2] especially with regard to the analyses of symbolic colonialism and construction of hegemonic masculinity through tourism and other leisure practices. While Davis remains unaware of the privileged class position affording her the leisure time in which to conduct research, the most compelling of which is threatened by the hyperbolic claim that it is upon the backs of the "entire (post)colonized world" that *SI* enlarges its purse, she certainly saves her best work for last. What makes her final analysis of the signifiers of exoticism in the swimsuit issue so interesting is the close attention paid to textual detail and her attempts to integrate symbolic and economic issues around the questions of the putative benefits of tourism and the demands of the tourist gaze. Davis decodes all of the stereotypes of cultural and racial differentiation of otherness at work over the years in the swimsuit issue, paying special attention to signifiers of inferiority (primitiveness, darkness, feminization and naturalization). She observes the uses of (post)colonialized others as exotic props, performers, natural born labourers, and the reservation of the sexual gaze for the ideal readers – media tourists and agents of symbolic colonialism – of the magazine back home in the West, that is, in the US and Canada, where almost all of *SI*'s subscribers live.

While Davis deftly skims from the text of the issue's preposterous and ridiculous references to shooting locations, especially in the West Indies, with their almost compulsory mention of Columbus, she doesn't connect motifs of discovery and invasion with the use of the swimsuit issue as a sexual voyage of mystification for adolescent boys. With no sense of a capitalist eros, Davis cannot place the publication on the boundary that it occupies between licit and forbidden forms of sexual representation, the very issue around which controversy about it swirls. Capital will forever try to peddle these representations which capture once and for all adolescent libido in heterosexual fantasies, simultaneously driving it to the consumption of more and more pin-ups, calendars, magazines, and videos, while directing it toward forbidden pleasures with which it likely will never have anything more than superficial contact.

What Davis' book fails to do is place the swimsuit issue in the culture of swimming, and of the beach and surf in the popular American imagination, not to mention representations of the sport of swimming. There is no mention of literary and cinematic evocations of swimming. Nothing about swimsuit competitions. And hardly anything about swimsuits.

Notes

1. My review of Laurel Davis, *The Swimsuit Issue and Sport: Hegemonic Masculinity in Sports Illustrated*, Albany: State University Press of New York, 1997, first appeared in *can* 1/1 (1998): 14-15.

2. Catherine Lutz and Jane Collins, *Reading National Geographic*, Chicago: The University of Chicago Press, 1993.

THE TWO ELVISES

Leather and

ice-skating are uneasy partners.[1] Kurt Browning, one may recall, reached for his leathers on occasion – but only a jacket. Elvis minor, that is, the Canadian figure skater Elvis (Stojko), has been known to wear a body-hugging, sleeveless leather pantsuit, with dramatic – one wants to say fetishistic with a clear nod to bondage rather than motorcycle chic – drawstrings on the pant legs. Stojko's outfit evokes Elvis major circa 1968, neck-to-toe in leather for his comeback television special, cookin' with his small combo – not to mention the famous photograph of him taken from *Jailhouse Rock*: the dancing, sneering, leather-clad prison rebel. Indeed, Elvis minor's Elvis Presley routine was not unveiled until after he had captured the World Championship in 1994. He had already startled the European competition with a martial arts-based routine choreographed to the music of Bruce Lee kung-fu films.

The thesis that pulls together Greil Marcus' collection of short essays on Elvis major, published as *Dead Elvis*, is twofold: Elvis tends to be buried under cultural ephemera, explained away, figured as an absence, as white trash, as someone who could not have meant to do what he did, on the grounds that he was not a "conscious cultural agent." It is the impossibility of Elvis as such an agent that Marcus challenges with the claim that he was "in a way that we don't quite understand" a conscious actor. There is something shaky about this possibility, something mysterious, and less than clear and distinct.

How, then, does Elvis minor keep himself from being buried under the mountains of paraphernalia? How does he remain, as it were, conscious? To play the symbol of the King – especially as a namesake, and the favourite performer of one's parents – is a dangerous business, for the risk is that a few souvenirs will lead to an associative avalanche: all of sudden, the fat jokes appear, the junky motif gets bandied around, someone remembers his fascination with the fourteen-year-old Priscilla, the jelly donuts … white trash accumulates quickly. Sure, when you're 1994 and 1995 World Figure Skating Champion (and ongoing Canadian Champion who, in his recent promotional work, helps teach Bobby Orr to skate, which is nothing short of heretical), all of this seems unlikely. Elvis minor: always in basic black, martial arts expert able to master the pain of his twisted ankle, never quick with a smile; the Olympic-sized winces, the signifiers of courage could not, even in Nagano, overcome the corruption motif of block judging. He is already widely known as the "King" of figure skating. It was, after all, the young Elvis – The King – who appeared by popular demand on the postage stamp. And it will be a young Elvis minor who sooner rather than later turns pro and joins his illustrious colleagues on the entertainment circuit. Viva Las Vegas? Boxing can be staged in a hotel parking lot. But can figure skating rule the desert?

Notes

1. The connection between leather and sexual/athletic performance is not confined to figure skating as the important example of Honor Blackman shows. It is possible to read her career in terms of the ligature of leather and judo through her fascinating text *Honor Blackman's Book of Self-Defence*, Harmondsworth: Penguin, 1967. There are two defining moments in Blackman's career, and both involved judo. The first hearkens back to her infamous performance as Pussy Galore in the James Bond film *Goldfinger*, in which she roughed up the secret agent himself; the second was her decision to dress in leather from the neck down in her role as Cathy Gale in the television series of the 1960s *The Avengers*, and at the same time to replace gun play with judo. In her book Blackman, sans leather, demonstrates in a series of staged photographs self-defence techniques against grope after grab after clutch, with pithy warnings such as "don't get too carried away by this one: if you use your full force on his elbow joint you'll probably break his arm and end up having to lend him cigarettes while you telephone for an ambulance." When smoking is heaped onto the leather-judo connection, the transgressive elements of Blackman's singular career become impossible to replicate; no remake could possibly capture it. In this mix the importance of smoking cannot be underestimated. The ensemble of cigarettes, martial arts and leather is supremely transgressive in the expanded field of sports.

ANALYTIC ESCAPADE

My colleague

Todd Dufresne and I have recently completed an investigation into the figure skating exploits of the well-known British psychoanalyst Ernest Jones.[1] Jones' book, *The Elements of Figure Skating*, was published in 1931, and a much expanded edition appeared in 1952; the latter included substantial analyses of such skating figures as Loops, Combination Steps, Mohawks/Choctaws, Grape Vines, an expanded section on Ice Dancing, and even an appendix on the "History of Skating." Long out of print and forgotten by historians of skating and psychoanalysis, Jones' *Elements* is testimony to his extraordinary para-professional passion for the sport. Besides the detailed, technical descriptions of skating figures, Jones ventured a psychology of skating in which psychoanalytic categories mixed with an erotics of the figures. Unfortunately, Jones never mentioned his lifelong passion for figure skating in his autobiography of 1959, *Free Associations*. His son Mervyn, however, was able to correct this oversight in an appended epilogue to the autobiography. Victor Brome, in his biography of Jones, expends little energy on Jones' interest in figure skating. However, Freud historian Paul Roazen, in a book on Helen Deutsch, pointed out that Deutsch admired Jones' breadth of interest, even though she had a personal distaste for him.

As Jones' son Mervyn has confirmed, his father was a bit of a rink rat. He was a member of The Ice Club on Grosvenor Road (which folded in 1939) and at Golder's Green in London. The elder Jones skated a great deal in the two years before the first edition of the

Elements appeared. A reading of his date books, which are found in the archives of The British Psycho-Analytical Society in London, reveal the rigours of his schedule and his failures. What is remarkable about Jones' work on skating is his innovation in the area of mistakes. For instance, Jones invented the phrase "life-saving stamp" – bringing one's free foot down to prevent a fall – and placed considerable emphasis on "the art of falling," that is, of "slithering" on ice. This interest without question reflects his own experiences. His date books record with astonishing exactitude his falls (their number and the injuries resulting from them) during his sessions. All of this practice, it should be said, was in preparation for the Third-Class National Skating Association Test. As he awaited the publication of his skating book, Jones took the test for the first time, while complaining of his "bad hips," in June of 1931. He scored nineteen points. He took the test again on December 17th, and scored only nineteen and a half points. The *Elements* was published on December 23rd. What Jones did not mention was the fact that a score of twenty (of a possible thirty-six) was a passing mark! Jones' love of the "ecstasy of motion" on ice outstripped, it is fair to say, his own mediocre technical skills. He was, however, by all accounts an excellent judge.

36

The skating club at the Grosvenor rink provided Jones with a number of contacts outside his psychoanalytic circles. For instance, Jones skated and was friends with Sir Stanley Unwin, who must have encouraged Jones to prepare a second edition of his book for Unwin's firm of Allen & Unwin. Jones' personal contact with the stars of the international skating world included Sonja Henie, Norwegian and World Champion, and star of ice dancing films (Henie's biography, *Wings on My Feet*, makes no mention of Jones). Notably, it is not a photograph of Henie that adorns the frontispiece of the first edition of *Elements*, it is rather a photograph of Miss Vivi-Anne Hultén, Lady Champion of Sweden.

It may also have been fateful that Jones skated with Sir Samuel Hoare, Home Secretary under Prime Minister Neville Chamberlain (1937-40). For according to a personal letter to Dr. Dufresne from Mervyn: "On a few occasions he [Jones] talked to Hoare at the club about visas for German and Austrian analysts who wanted to come to Britain and, congratulating Hoare on his skating (Hoare was a vain man), persuaded him to grant the visas." Hoare was, in fact, the mysterious "skating friend" to whom Jones referred in his letters to Vienna during his successful efforts in getting a number of analysts out of occupied Austria, including Sigmund Freud.

Orthodox clinicians of whatever stripe will bristle at such investigations. Against the conservatism of psychoanalysis, they appear undisciplined. And they are, in an entirely salutary sense. For they lift the veil of the everyday life of psychoanalysis, revealing the para-professional passions that worked their way into the theory and practice, and vice versa. Jones' skating books, Marie Bonaparte's book about her chow-chow Topsy, Freud's toys (collection of antiquities) and his own puppy loves: this real stuff of psychoanalytic history has nothing to do with the whitewashed official biographies and museums displays. Sensing the strange attraction between psychoanalysis and athletics, art critic Jeanne Randolph proffered a fiction called "Psychoanalysis and Synchronized Swimming" in which she is a chlorinated, muscular, smiling adept, although the Toronto Psycho-Analytic Society will have none of it:

> *We are having trouble following you. And, in fact,*
> *do not follow you at all.*
> *Do you want me to go through it step by step again? I had asked.*
> *Frankly, we simply are not prepared to go along with you on this,*
> *at all, ever.*
> *Go along with me? What are we doing, psychoanalysis or*
> *synchronized swimming?* [2]

Notes

1. Todd Dufresne and Gary Genosko, "Jones on Ice: Psychoanalysis and Figure Skating," *International Journal of Psycho-Analysis* 76 (1995): 123-33.

2. Jeanne Randolph, "Psychoanalysis and Synchronized Swimming," in *Psychoanalysis and Synchronized Swimming, and other writings on art*, Toronto: YYZ, 1991, p. 151.

A MARS BAR A DAY

The official

weigh-in of contenders is an event enshrined in boxing culture, as is the official weigh-out for jockeys and saddles in horse racing. Ian Hamilton's remarkable portrait of the English foot-baller Paul Gascoigne (Gazza), "Gazza Agonistes" (*Granta* 45, 1993) makes of weight a weighty matter. Hamilton's alimentary tract monitors Gazza's weight: gained, lost, regained. Written with the clinical eye of a fan, Hamilton's work opens onto a cultural code of bad food and manners. It is all the more timely in light of Gazza's release from England's national team on the eve of the 1998 World Cup. He had, it appears, slipped out on too many occasions for a kebab.

Hamilton first noticed Gazza when he was playing for Newcastle, and follows him through his sale to Tottenham, and then to Lazio (Rome), and in several World Cups along the way (from, then, roughly 1987-1993). Gazza was a "noticeably fat" child whose layers survived into his teens as "puppy fat." Taunts of "Fat Boy" and "Fattie" followed him throughout his career as he became somewhat notorious for gaining weight in the off-season and when he was sidelined with his many injuries. Gazza would claim that he was never really as fat as everyone thought since "the English papers used to touch the pictures up to look fatter." Gazza claimed, in fact, he played better when he was "a little overweight." He would occasionally lapse into culinary racism with reference to his Gallic roots, hoping aloud that he would never start eating "snails and garlic."

Hamilton is ever attentive to Gazza's preferences: McDonald's, Mars Bars, pizza, pasta, mozzarella cheese, steak, chips, beer. After being sold to Tottenham in 1988, the first time Gazza returned there with his new team he was "bombarded with frozen Mars Bars." The Mars Bar has a remarkable semiotic vehicularity in English culture. In the spring of 1994 in London, a public health nurse involved in the sex education of prepubescent girls caused a media sensation when she related that one of her students had asked her to explain what was meant by a "Mars Bar party." The fact of her explanation caused a furor. No one reported what it was that she explained, although the press lingered over the notion for weeks. The Mars Bar became a fetish, an overvalued object that substitutes for another's sexuality. What are we to make of the shower of Mars Bars? Clearly, in Gazza's absence from Newcastle, he could be adored through the fetish of the Mars Bar which he, as Hamilton tells us, adored. The Mars Bar did not so much take the place of Gazza, but rather, was violently returned to him, as if to say in a collective voice: the symbolic connection with you through the Mars Bar is unsatisfactory: why did you leave us? We hate you for it! And you can stick this Mars Bar … ! Which is precisely what happened. Who is our very own Gazza? Why, it's Nancy Greene, the Canadian skiing hero of distant Olympic lore who was for so many years a spokesperson for Mars Bars.

There is also the matter of the belch: *Il commento gastrico.* Pursued by Italian television reporters and cameras into the parking lot behind Stadio Olympico in Rome, Gazza broke one of his periodic silences in the face of the press with what Hamilton describes as, with evident delight, "a belch: nothing Falstaffian, more a side-of-the-mouth hiccup, but unmistakably non-verbal." The belch played better in the Italian media than in England, where it became a semiotic object worthy of a Barthesean mythological analysis. A belch, a smack on the knee with a tire iron, a sweet taste of Benadryl (remember Canadian rower Silken Laumann's seemingly innocent dosage?): transgressions like these make headlines and, in their wake, reports write themselves. Isn't this belch the logical consequence of Gazza's diet, a coupla burgers and a few jars? While Hamilton was amused by many of the belch-related articles that appeared, he gave vent to his incredulity with regard to one, written "by a professor of 'cultural studies' at Lancaster" for the *Daily Mail* – not exactly a quality newspaper, but one wise to the inevitability of academics going tabloid – concerning "the 'new Englishman' who was 'increasingly being seen as a brutish and leering figure with little or no right to respect'." In other words, the football hooligan: full of gas, racist slurs, and fascist tendencies. A frozen Mars Bar, after all, is a lethal weapon when thrown from a great height.

OBITUARY NOTICE

On August

29, 1995, Jeff Z. Klein and Andrew Hsiao, who were *Village Voice* sports editors for 1993-95 and 1992-93 respectively, penned their own epitaph as the paper ended its sports coverage.[1] Since 1983 the *Voice* had cultivated, as they put it, "an irreverent, progressive point of view" on sports. Race, gender, labour – did I mention queer – issues were all part of this unique reportage that blazed a trail for cultural studies of sport in North America. Whether cultural studies in its American incarnation will pick up the trail remains as yet unanswered, although indications are strong that it will, despite the recent remarks of those such as Elliot Gorn who, in an editorial in the *Chronicle of Higher Education* (24 March 1995) claimed that "the booming field of cultural studies seems oblivious to the work done on athletics. This is ironic, because cultural studies … is exactly where the study of sports is most needed." An exception is Michael Oriard's *Reading Football*, a study of football's cultural narratives (the gladiator, "scientific" football, heroic masculinity, etc.) in the popular journalism of the late nineteenth and early twentieth centuries.[2]

There were treasures to be discovered in the *Voice* sports columns (the gossipy "Jockbeat" and Mike Geffner's baseball report, "Rundown"), and the one or two articles presented in each issue. For example, I was staggered by the implications for research of the recent casual cultural history in the *Voice* by Gersh Kuntzman (*VV* 11 July 1995) of the "high-five" celebratory gesture in baseball, which turns out to constitute a rhizome crossing baseball and college basketball, involving the mutation of handshakes, butt-slaps, low fives ("giving skin"), high fives proper, high tens, the full moon, and the forearm bash (recalling with neanderthal enthusiasm the fist bash).

Where do we go from here? Specifically, a comparative analysis of the history and meaning of the celebratory gesture across sports remains to be written, in the context of a broader study of gestural sporting behaviour (of athletes and fans alike – "the wave" being a prime example, as well as the waving of all sorts of gimmicky objects such as "Homer Hankies" in baseball, and in hockey, the long-standing tradition in Detroit of throwing octopuses onto the ice), as regrettable as this may be at times (such as the racist "tomahawk chop" used by Atlanta Braves fans and widely protested by Native American and other groups). In hockey, equipment imposes a set of what may be called syntactic constraints upon innovation. Within these confines, one may recall retired Maple Leaf and Canuck Dave "Tiger" Williams' celebratory rush down the ice, arms pumping, as he shifted his stick backwards between his legs in order to ride it like a hobby horse, not to mention all the usual fist pumping, air punching, stick swinging, twirling, embracing, patting, petting, and rubbing, etc. A photograph of Canadian journalist Daniel Gawthrop astride his stick is clearly a reference to the Tiger rather than a phallic stick, perhaps a broomstick. The best part of this decoding is that one doesn't have to be a Canucks fan to understand it.

Indeed, the pickings are slim and in Canada almost nonexistent, the exceptions being few and far between – one thinks immediately of Daniel Gawthrop's queer hockey and sports reportage in *Xtra West* and elsewhere, as well as material generated by the political and fiscal follies of the drive to save the Winnipeg Jets.[3]

Generally, for the progressive reader of sports – even though, as Nick Hornby reminds us, the word progressive has, for the some of us, the unfortunate connotation of the music of King Crimson and Emerson, Lake and Palmer – the solution is to become a writer.

Notes

1. "Game Over," *Village Voice* (29 August 1995).

2. Michael Oriard, *Reading Football: How the Popular Press Created an American Spectacle*, Chapel Hill: University of North Carolina Press, 1993.

3. Gawthrop's pieces in the *Vancouver Sun*, *Xtra West*, and accounts of his exploits in *LA Weekly*, *Globe & Mail* and *Village Voice* during 1992-93 constitute a remarkable episode in Canadian sports culture.

RESURRECTED

In 1995

I posted an obituary notice for the *Village Voice's* sports section in my *Borderlines* column. Well, after a year and a half, it's alive. "Hello, Lazarus!" as sports editor Brian Parks puts it. "The Score," as the sports section is now called, cannot recapture the irreverent reportage of its former staff, most of whom were lost in the *Voice* purges of '95. Remember that the credo of the sports section under the direction of its previous editors was, among all the many other things it had going for it, pro-union. A sobering thought in times such as these when the dumb are inheriting the earth.

THANATOLOGY

"When a

boxer is 'knocked out' it does not mean, as it's commonly thought, that he has been knocked unconscious, or even incapacitated; it means rather more poetically that he has been knocked out of Time. (The referee's dramatic count of ten constitutes a metaphysical parenthesis of a kind through which the fallen boxer must pass if he hopes to continue in Time.)," writes Joyce Carol Oates in her collection of essays *On Boxing*.[1] To be out of time is to be counted dead. The knock out constitutes a symbolic death with its own rhythm: the count of one to ten. To resist this rhythm and re-enter time, continuing the bout, is to return from the dead; succumbing to this rhythm and letting it run its course brings the fight to an end. Let's note that this symbolic death is embedded in the rules of the sport, it is a dramatic part of the ritual. Despite being extratemporal, it is not altogether separate for this death takes place in the ring. It is for good reason that Oates uses the concept of parentheses (which are neither the brackets of phenomenology nor the diacritical playmakers of deconstruction) to describe the knock out. This turns the referee into a kind of priest with exclusive control over a restricted domain. It is by means of the referee's power to mediate between the temporal and extratemporal, between the living and symbolically dead, that a boxer can return from the dead. The referee mediates the communication between the living and dead. These symbolically dead boxers have a crucial role to play in the match because, in boxing, it is normal to be, in this way, dead. And this is what is extraordinary about boxing: death is not spirited away and dressed up for viewing, but remains in circulation amongst the living who are simultaneously repulsed and fascinated by everything that happens in the parentheses. Boxing's refusal to either repress death or to hide it away in an extraterritorial space also explains why it is reviled by so many, without investigating other reasons such as its interminable scams and scandals, alleged mob connections, and violent spillovers of every kind.

The history of boxing is littered with real thanatopraxis as well, in the ring itself, and the slow death of the retired boxer. Every time a "bum of the month" is produced from the ranks to face a superior opponent, every time a match is allowed to go on a few seconds too long before being stopped, every time a boxer suffers a career-ending injury, death hovers over the ring. For boxing does not refuse the boxer his death; it does not have the power to suspend death, for the boxer's death is always at stake, and this is especially true in mismatches in which a boxer is not properly protected by his handlers, and in the strategy adopted by a fighter, such as the innovative but physically costly rope-a-dope introduced by Muhammad Ali against George Foreman in Zaire in 1974. The rules do not prevent a violent death from being at stake.

What about blood? In boxing, death is not a simulated spectacle, despite the cries of "kill him" and "murder the guy" that are crowd noises in a soundtrack of pain. Blood is boxing's spectacle, and it has been suggestively exploited in films such as Martin Scorsese's *Raging Bull* (1980). It was Scorsese who showed how blood could spray like a geyser from around the nose of the boxer in the figure of Jake La Motta, the one who did not fear death. The ring scenes of *Raging Bull* were carefully choreographed by professional boxers. What an extraordinary advance these scenes represent beyond those choreographed by Sylvester Stallone in John Avildsen's *Rocky* (1976). Stallone's character the Italian Stallion simply does not block a punch; he is, after all, more at home punching sides of beef in a slaughterhouse freezer. The shots he takes at these carcasses, ultimately breaking ribs and mushing prime cuts, are signifiers of death in contrast to the puppies, goldfish and turtles he loves, and the clerk in the pet shop he pursues romantically; in the end, Adrian, Rocky's girlfriend, is admitted into the family. *Rocky* has a bestiary whose devalued members are slaughtered, butchered, and hung in the freezer. True, Rocky has blood on his hands, but not because he is a killer; rather, he beats up on what is already dead.

Blood is the cinematic subject of *Tokyo Fist* (Shinya Tsukamoto, 1995). The concussive blows and frenetic boxing scenes pay homage to the most ferocious moments of *Raging Bull*, to be sure, and there are three obvious quotations: the boxer Tsuda smashes his head against the cement wall of a highway underpass in the same manner as La Motta against the wall of his prison cell; the geyser of blood from the face of Kojima, Tsuda's high school friend, sparring partner, and enemy, shot in profile, revisits this motif; finally, the slow motion waves of blood pouring from the eye of Tsuda in his hospital bed recall Scorsese's use of rippling and running water (over the legs of La Motta's wife-to-be in the swimming pool, and from the sponge used to moisten the boxer's body in the corner of the ring). Blood is the fountain of death and it is brilliantly simulated in the cinematic representations of boxing in the work of Scorsese and Tsukamoto. It may even be said that the pulverized faces of Tsukamoto's boxers pay homage to the broken sides of beef beaten into raw mash by Rocky.

Notes
1. Joyce Carol Oates, *On Boxing*, Hopewell, N.J.: The Ecco Press, 1994, p. 15.

THE LOUISVILLE LIP

Elliott Gorn,

professor of American Studies at Miami University in Ohio, has lamented the lack of attention given to sports by students of cultural studies. With the publication of his edited collection, *Muhammad Ali: The People's Champ*, he comes across with the goods.[1] Ali may have believed that Jack Johnson was the greatest fighter of all time, but for Gorn, Ali was truly the greatest. It needs to be kept in mind that Miles Davis' soundtrack to William Clayton's documentary of 1970, *Jack Johnson*, is a jazz fusion juggernaut that has no equivalent in the Ali camp – at least not yet. Ali once refused an offer to play Jack Johnson in a Hollywood version of his life story. And rightly so, for Martin Ritt's film *The Great White Hope* (1970), starring James Earl Jones, is a pathetic spectacle that contains very little boxing; in fact, the very absence of fight scenes in a fight film makes the work strangely fascinating.

Ali's career remains a contested text. His athletic accomplishments were political issues, sometimes provocations. His personal life was a political minefield. The explosions began when he changed his name upon converting to Islam (let's not forget that with the murder of Malcolm X in 1965, Ali became the most visible minister of the Nation of Islam, even if Elijah Muhammad would suspend him in the late 1960s just as his boxing career was being revived – it wasn't until the mid-1970s that Ali was accepted back into the Nation's fold); indeed, Ali was not alone given that major black figures in sport such as Lew Alcindor (basketball) and Bobby Moore (football) had done the same upon converting to Islam. Ali also raised the political consciousness of black athletes during the Olympic boycott/protest of 1968 directed against the participation of South Africa. Perhaps most significantly, Ali's opposition to the Vietnam War precipitated a legal struggle with the American government that lasted five years (1966-1971) and cost him the heavyweight championship. He returned to the ring in 1970 to defeat Jerry Quarry, dubbed "the great white hope." Thus began his ascent to the title that he would recapture in 1974 with his stunningly orchestrated defeat of the younger and larger George Foreman. It was then that Ali, speaking to James Earl Jones who portrayed Johnson (renamed Jack Jefferson) in the film *The Great White Hope*, understood that his experience was parallel with that of Johnson's, and that the sixty-odd years that separated them had not changed the racism they encountered (Johnson had to defend the heavyweight title he won in 1908 against a White Hope contender). The "white hope" is a staple figure in boxing; yet Ali had eschewed, for religious and political reasons, the flamboyant lifestyle that Johnson adopted in his acquisition and display, as one contributor notes, of "white prerogatives." Ali's sexism, his work for the Reagan campaign, and even his efforts to "re-gender" boxing with claims of his own prettiness and the poetry that issued from his busy lips ("float like a butterfly, sting like a bee"), are all brought into critical focus.

What these readings of Ali teach – despite the misgivings of one of the contributors – is that boxing is not removed by any representational device, whether it is by reflection or refraction, from race politics. The "race card" is not played in relation to boxing as if it was somehow separate. Boxing is a political medium, and race (alongside death) is one of its constitutive features.

Notes

1. Elliot Gorn's edited edition *Muhammad Ali: The People's Champ*, was published by the University of Illinois Press in 1995. For a more recent example of the investigation of boxing as visual culture see *BOXER: An Anthology of Writings on Boxing and Visual Arts,* Cambridge, Mass. and London: The MIT Press and The Institute of International Visual Arts, 1996. This is an extraordinary document combining lively academic essays, historical documents and contemporary visual arts around the theme of boxing. The discussions are wide-ranging and right on target: representations of women in boxing, the buying and training of Mike Tyson, the exploits of poet, boxer, and surrealist dandy, Arthur Cravan, as well as an erotics of the ring read through the cinema; as Jake La Motta confusedly said in *Raging Bull* upon seeing a pretty opponent: "I don't know whether to fight him or fuck him."

On the topic of boxing I should not neglect to mention the Australian magazine *Philosopher* (PO Box 232, Northbridge, NSW, Australia 2063). Despite the tired and pedantic tone of some of the articles, a recent issue considered the boxer as moral hero with valuable reminders of the history of reflections on this sport in the Greek tradition, in Homer and Plato, right up to the stirring metaphysical confabulations of Ali himself. Not exactly an intellectual dust-up worthy of the topic, but a good wedge with which to get the sport into the curriculum.

REVENGE OF THE PIGSKIN

After the

sterling vulgarity of yet another Super Bowl Sunday – a spectacle designed, after all, for those denied access to the *jouissance* of capitalist elites, and an event highly productive of a wide range of personal problems, making it a boon to the caring professions as well as to advertisers, it is therapeutic to reflect on the football experiences in Don DeLillo's much neglected novel *End Zone*.[1] Enigmatic running back Gary Harkness, whose strange behaviour at other, major colleges, qualifies him, in the eyes of the coach, to be a leader at the tiny and obscure Logos College, has a passion for scenarios of nuclear destruction. These scenarios are closely related to pass and defense patterns on the gridiron, which he treats with theological concern. *End Zone* is the portrait of a footballer as a young metaphysician. One day, the kicker Bing Jackman relates a strange insight to Harkness, the only one to whom such an unbelievable thing could be told: "I sensed knowledge in the football. I sensed a strange power and restfulness. The football possessed awareness. The football knew what was happening. It knew. I'm sure of it." The real question, Harkness adds, is not whether the football was aware of its footballness, but whether it was aware of its awareness. Self-awareness is set against the football's objecthood in DeLillo's postmodern theory of the object. Stop joking around, Jackman says. This is not the alienation of commodity fetishism, but what makes the game seductive: the discovery of a hidden rule.

This rule is the only compensation there can be for the nonstop contest of Super Sunday.

Notes

1. Don DeLillo, *End Zone*, New York: Simon & Schuster, 1972.

THE PROTAGONIST

La rondelle,

the hockey puck, is a feminine noun; but *le base-ball* is masculine. Despite this, in hockey and baseball circles in North America, at least, pucks and baseballs are not thought of as gendered objects; frankly, and banally, the puck is an it, and no amount of emphasis connecting it with Shakespeare's Puck from *A Midsummer Night's Dream* will imbue it with gendered – possessing or bending – mischief. It can be passed around to no end and even received with soft hands, but it is still a black rubber thing, even when women play with it; nobody says "s/he's as cold and hard as a puck," although they might. The comedian Don Rickles, allegedly a Canadian, made a career out of insulting people by calling them a "hockey puck," a rather thinly veiled racist epithet that went over alarmingly well in the newly minted bedroom communities that grew up around Canadian cities in the 1960s. On the whole, informal language has not made much of the vulcanization process and its employment of sulphur. It would take a leap of Freudian faith to suggest that the ring in ringette was, symbolically speaking, feminine.

However, as Eduardo Galeano explains in *Soccer in Sun and Shadow*, elsewhere things are quite different: "In Brazil, no one doubts the ball is a woman. Brazilians call her pudgy, *gorduchinha*, or baby, *menina*, and they give her names like Maricota, Leonor or Margarita."[1] She is at times loyal, a quality she shares with the Canadian football, known to take a bounce – an Argo bounce – for the homeside; yet, she is fickle, as anyone who has ever seen a sure goal slowly curve away from an open net knows. In this regard hockey puts too much faith in the goalposts and crossbar, making them the true protagonists of the drama around the net. The soccer ball, however, is easily offended by unnecessary roughness. It knows it can break hearts and this makes it vain. Before the invention of the stitchless ball the question of vanity was not as compelling, but afterwords, well, it is inescapable, and tantamount to the removal of braces. A puck is a frozen object in more ways than one: literally cold, hard, limited in characteristics susceptible to personification; sure, it may stand on its edge once in a while, and adhere to the stick of the Great One, but it lacks the lightness, the air, and the inflated ego to be sure, of the soccer ball. A puck is frozen into submission. When it takes an erratic bounce, this is barely tolerated wantonness.

On several occasions Galeano mentions that the ball may be lulled to sleep on the foot. In his description of "the idol," for instance, he writes: "The ball seeks him out, knows him, needs him. She rests and rocks him on the top of his foot." Like a woman asleep in a crescent moon, the ball rests on the foot of the great player. In describing the idol, Galeano cannot refrain from describing the ball, her character and qualities. He knows this offends the major- 51 ity of Leftist intellectuals for whom soccer is a circus without bread and the ball a hypnotizing woman who exercizes a "perverse fascination" for workers, leading them around like a femme fatale. One may recall Trotsky's criticisms of the uncertain "athletic stunts" of poet Mayakovsky. Galeano knows that once upon a time the Left did not denigrate the game, suggesting that the great Italian Marxist intellectual "Antonio Gramsci praised 'this open-aired kingdom of human loyalty'."

In 1998, the year of the home-run ball when not one but two players broke Roger Maris' record, the prospect of getting the actual record-breaking ball from the bat of McGwire and/ or Sosa created a certain amount of pandemonium. In the name of authenticity and crowd control, specially marked balls were used. Nobody wanted the ball to disappear. And no one in the commissioner's office wanted to deal with all the charlatans, the fake baseballs, the claims and counter-claims. And it worked well enough. The violence and desperation in the stands, while still a mob scene, was quelled. Sure, there were a few bloodied noses, a threatened lawsuit or two, and bad feelings about the trampling some people received, but the process was streamlined, and a collector's item was neatly fashioned in advance, and readied for auction. What major league baseball didn't count on was the publication of Don DeLillo's latest novel *Underworld*.

All of a sudden, the shot heard around the world – the home run by the New York Giants' Bobby Thompson off of Ralph Branca at the Polo Grounds that brought the Giants' the pennant in 1951 – was again on the agenda. Major league baseball could not control the mystery around that baseball. Having acquainted himself with the mysteries of footballs in his earlier work, DeLillo went to work manufacturing a story, not around the event, but in light of the ball and the question of its destiny. The issue is the ball's uncertain lineage. It is hard to establish because the trail runs cold in the backwards-looking gaze of memorabiliaists. Not even the "ESP of baseball," into which one collector in the novel is sensitively attuned, can help overcome the gap, the tear in the narrative into which the ball rolled; it's only one day but it makes all the difference in the world.

DeLillo's version of events is hyper-ordinary. A boy skips school, sneaks into the game, happens to sit in the section where the ball lands, manages to wrestle the home-run ball away from several larger men, one of whom pursues him, and brings it home. He relates the tale to his father, a small-time hustler, who takes it from him and sells it to a man who is waiting for playoff tickets to go on sale outside the stadium with his son. The ball is sold for thirty-two dollars and change. It cannot be sold for more because of a twofold legitimation crisis: the man with the ball is black. It's not just a matter of explaining what he has in his possession to the ball club; it would be an explanation coming from an unemployed black man. He sells it to a white father sleeping overnight with his son in the line for playoff tickets, to be precise. The deal is a tragic one. The buyer believes the ball is real and empties his pockets (well, without sacrificing the ticket money), as well as his flask of Irish whiskey. Buyer beware, DeLillo quips, because the ball eventually passes into the hands of the white father's son for whom it means nothing. He is the missing link in the ball's lineage and cannot be located, even though the rest of its subsequent owners have been traced. The ball must have been the real thing because it had a green smudge, the colour of the pillar in the Polo Grounds off which it bounced. The encrypted sign on the McGwire ball has replaced the uncertain smudge, the genuine sign of contiguity with the stadium itself, in the game of collecting. This represents nothing less than the triumph of accountancy over the interpretation of uncertain signs and the obsessive research of fans and collectors. The proof of authenticity becomes abstract, removed from the conditions on a particular day, in a particular theatre of baseball. The McGwire ball was already statistically entombed before it was hit. It will never sit "wrapped in tissue paper inside an old red-and-white Spalding box."[2] DeLillo's "small white innocent object" injects uncertainty into the formulaic celebrations of baseball today by reminding us of another ball's destiny, and the more general question of the wiliness of sporting objects.

Notes

1. Eduardo Galeano, *Soccer in Sun and Shadow*, London: Verso, 1998, p. 21. See also Sam Pryke, "Offside! Contemporary Artists and Football," *Third Text* 36 (1996): 102-4. The exhibition contained a photograph and descriptive text by Crispin Jones of one of the leather soccer balls that Captain W.P. Neville distributed to four platoons at the Battle of the Somme in 1916 in order to see who would be the first to kick it into the German trenches. Pryke reminds us that some 21, 000 British soldiers died in this battle.

2. Don DeLillo, *Underworld*, New York: Scribner, 1997, p. 177. The more radical question is whether the home-run record would have been broken in the absence of the impetus provided by the DeLillo novel. Indeed, who is the anonymous owner of the most famous piece of baseball memorabilia, the so-called Babe Ruth baseball, which recently sold for $126, 500? This is small potatoes, of course, when compared to the McGwire ball.

GIRLJOCKS

"The equation,"

Victoria A. Brownworth explains in her contribution, "The Competitive Closet," to *Sportsdykes*, "has always been simplistic: sports are masculine; women in sports are masculine; therefore, women in sports are lesbians."[1] Simplistic, but not simple: sports training masculinizes women's bodies, but this does not make them lesbians. The simplistic logic of the argument (and the punitive models of femininity it implies) has fuelled the dyke-baiting which has haunted women's sports for decades. Consider the LPGA (Ladies Professional Golf Association), which has been the target of such baiting and misogynist ranting since its inception in 1950. The LPGA continues to be stigmatized by the male sportswriting establishment because one of its founders, Babe Didrikson, had well-known affairs with other women on the tour. Today, nothing has changed, if one considers the recent example of CBS golf analyst Ben Wright, whose homophobic and misogynist tirades were widely reported. One such report by Mary Jollimore in the *Globe & Mail* (4 December 1995) thought it sufficient to let him hang himself, thus missing the opportunity to expose the fact that opinions like his – not to mention decisions like hers – have been replayed for some five decades. One positive lesson is that an episode like this one puts into relief the significance of *Sportsdykes* in which several of the contributors directly confront the deleterious effects (on the careers of individual women and, ultimately, on everyone in the sportscape) of all kinds of sexual stereotyping of women athletes.

While one never tires of revisiting the quite different episodes of the coming out of such stars as Martina Navratilova and Billie Jean King, *Sportsdykes* maps out the personal meanings of these events for couch potatoes and young athletes alike. An entire section is devoted to "Our Heroines, or, Martina," and it is here that Joan Hilty's comic strip "Viva Barcelona" appears, first published in *GirlJock* magazine – an important source for material – telling the story of a couch potato who becomes a spike-head during the summer Olympics, falling in love with the US women's volleyball team, as her "gaydar" constantly goes off – which wouldn't be necessary if there were more openly gay athletes. But this would require a revolution in sports and the sooner, the better, as the contributors to *Sportsdykes* testify.

Notes

1. Victoria A. Brownworth, "The Competitive Closet," in *Sportsdykes*, Susan Fox Rogers (ed.), New York: St. Martin's, 1994, p. 80.

HELL ON WHEELS

The sportscape

is under renovation. New types of institutional sporting facilities are appearing in the forms of skateparks, with their Gaudi-esque contours and graffitied bowls, colossal indoor snowboarding ramps plastered with trucked-in snow like raves on ice, and rock gyms in the gutted boiler rooms of industrial buildings. Existing single-use leisure sites such as ski slopes are being invaded by snowboarders, bicycle paths and lanes are full of in-line skaters, and drained swimming pools are haunted by skateboarders. While the sportscape is changing, it is also being generalized. The sportscape is the city itself. Just as mountain bikers surmounted to some degree certain obstacles of the streetscape, culminating in the kamikaze subculture of the bike courier, skateboarders and in-line skaters are rediscovering these and other obstacles – curbs, stairs, hand and guard rails, gaps, edges, trashbins, parked cars, benches – and turning them into the found tools of street skating. This is urban studies on wheels. Surrealists and situationists may have perfected urban drifting, but boarders and skaters are refinishing the cityscape with streetstyle highjinks by grinding on rails, pipes, and ledges of all sorts, riding walls or flying over vehicles after being launched by jump ramps. Postwar North American youth culture has, after all, always favoured wheels of some sort, and inevitably took some heat for the way they were used, from the days of drag racers in the late 1940s, street cruising in the 1950s, motorcycle cults of the 1960s, three and six wheel off-road buggies in the 1970s, the rise of the mountain bike and return of the Jeep in the 1980s and now, the era of the little wheels.

Amid the torrent of new magazines swamping the racks – derisively misidentified as the first efforts of twenty-somethings – are the print vehicles of skateboarding, in-line skating and snowboarding cultures. Print, let's say, is still alive and well and seething at the bottom, despite the Conrad Black-blood clots at the top. Notwithstanding the venerable *Thrasher*, which is celebrating its fifteenth anniversary,[1] most skateboarding titles such as *Slap* and *Blur* are relatively young, four years to be precise. *Thrasher* and *Slap* are products of San Francisco, while *Blur* is published in Portland, Oregon, with one editor in Brooklyn, New York. *In Line Skating Magazine*, from Boulder, Colorado, is into its fifth volume, while the "franglais" *Asphalte* of Montréal is barely two years old (this is the only magazine I have seen that prints a disclaimer in the table of contents warning readers: "Some of the pictures in this magazine show dangerous stunts. Skaters on pictures are professionals. We do not recommand [sic] that beginners try these tricks." All of the pitfalls are, in a sense, already in this statement). What makes *Asphalte* unique is its unpostured retro feel achieved through an anti-slickness that only underfunding can sustain – not to mention the lingering sensation of a nitrate rush at a roller disco. The snowboarding magazine *Stick* is part of Ray Gun Publishing from Santa Monica, California. Whether or not it was pure hyperbole or the irrepressible energy of the premier issue, *Stick* claims that snowboarding is "the new rock 'n' roll." Some pop musical reference is compulsory in these magazines since the subjectivities of boarders and skaters are woven into and augmented by styles ranging from hardcore punk to ambient: "Peace. Skate and destroy," as they say.

Youth culture on boards and wheels is only superficially reducible to style alone and is as compromised as any economically driven sporting culture. Such a desultory analysis would, however, miss the contestations expressed in the pages of these magazines. While bad attitudes abound towards sponsored events such as ESPN's Extreme Games and every mainstream recuperation of skateboarding, attitude is not the end of it. Admittedly, there is no sustained critique of cooptation and banalization. *Thrasher* and *Slap* simply reproduce themselves through their name brand paraphernalia, as do numerous board, boot, wheel, clothing and record companies who advertise in their pages and sponsor events and individuals. Skaters and riders of the year, both men and women, are crowned and celebrated through

57

profiles. While women are beginning to gain full recognition in competitive terms in what has been a boy's universe, they rarely appear as sponsored professionals in the product advertising that drives the magazines and defines the material signscape, the stuff of skate- and snowboarding. Editorial exceptions include *Stick's* largely pictorial profile of snowboarder Wendy Powell, *In Line Skating's* cover story on #1 vert skater Tasha Hodgson – who has her own pro wheel, which is no mean feat – and *Asphalte's* bio of Laura Connery, a Canadian vert skater who placed third at the Extreme Games and has several sponsorships and video credits to her name (video is a significant market for in-line skaters and skateboarders). Karina Pourreaux, "editrice" of *Asphalte*, highlights women's accomplishments and takes notice of training organizations such as FAAST (Female Amateur Aggressive Skating Team) in Toronto. Recognition attained through product and team sponsorship is critical to becoming professional even if subcultural elements are compromised in the process.

Will women become more and more identified with the material and semiotic cultures of these activities, and to what effects? At this stage, women primarily occupy modelling roles in Label Whore and Calvin ads, and misogyny is tied to predatory adolescent male desire and the normalized naming of weakness as feminine and genital. The immediate outlook is neither promising nor radical, even though new e-zines are emerging such as *Fresh and Tasty*, aimed at women snowboarders; this welcome development doesn't displace the gnarly moves of all the young dudes, especially our own doobie brother and cyber-star Ross Rebagliati. But for those rising women stars who are in their early to mid-twenties and still living at home, independence can appear to be gained through their chosen sports with successful sponsorships. Alas, this also ensnares women and their sporting sub-cultural lifestyles in the well-known traps of seeking fulfillment through commercial means. Every time we see Tasha Hodgson, a Senate logo is nearby, and the revolving design treadmill beckons. In the early 1960s, Tom Wolfe described teen hot rod culture in *The Kandy-Kolored Tangerine-Flake Streamline Baby* as a little anti-establishment world on the way to being hypnotized by the "huge asinine picture of themselves, which they were sure to like," drawn especially for them by the establishment. There isn't a boarding or skating television sitcom just as yet (notwithstanding the doping scandal at Nagano and motherly advice served on cue by neo-con luncheonette Jan Wong), but the set is warming up.

Street hassles around the use of public space are key to the representations of skateboarding and blading cultures. Snowboarding is, in this regard, snowbound. Picture Mike Davis, author of *City of Quartz* and *Ecology of Fear*, both examinations of Los Angeles, on a skateboard, in a downtown public square where skating is banned, nosegrinding on a bench, and you get the picture. The heat will be on him like an electric blanket. *Slap* builds a two-page spread around a quote from *City of Quartz* to make its point about the oppositional nature of skateboarding. The theme of "deconstruct" drives a similar eight-page pictorial series of urban exploits, and a report on the skating ban in downtown San Jose hits their mean streets. At the end of an interview with skater of the year Chris Senn, *Thrasher* pictures him taking some heat from The Man after exploiting a hand rail at San Francisco State. *Blur's* on-site introductory op-ed piece ends when the cops converge on Astor Place in New York City and scatter the skaters. Only apolitical postmodernists leave their gear at home before hitting the street. It's hell on wheels.

Notes

1. This article was originally written in early 1996 and all the magazines mentioned are from this period. 59 The number of magazines has continued to grow along with e-zines and web sites devoted to the sport.

THE JOY OF DEFEAT

Undisciplined

60 sociologist Jean Baudrillard loves radical losers.[1] In several remarkable and hitherto completely neglected pages at the end of *For a Critique of the Political Economy of the Sign*, he cites examples of athletes whose fame rests on their "chronic incapacity to wrap up victory." It makes little difference for Baudrillard whether an athlete has a knack for losing – through "slips of the will," as he puts it – or is a perennial runner-up, or is even irresistibly drawn to blowing it. Regardless of whether the loss in question is accidental or deliberate, what Baudrillard appreciates about these losers is that something keeps them from winning, something that makes their failure successful, and conversely, would turn victory into failure. Against the drive to satisfaction and the imperative of performance, of being all you can be, as the militarists tell us, Baudrillard theorizes failure: it is a matter of nothing less than the ability to sell oneself short against all rational demands to do otherwise. This is not merely a masochistic reversal of achievement, Baudrillard insists, but a more fundamental questioning of desire itself and the conditions of its fulfillment. These losers are ambivalent about the performance and perfection imperatives and the will to win. They refuse such fulfillment and satisfaction in order to preserve their own truth by not reproducing the competitive value system in which victory, placing, and even making the team can be exchanged for personal satisfaction and profit. Radical losers throw a wrench into the so-called good works of their sponsors. Baudrillard considers Tony Richardson's 1962 film, *The Loneliness of the Long-Distance Runner* (the screen

version of Alan Sillitoe's short story from 1959 of the Borstal Boy who throws away victory) to be a prime example of intentional failure as a form of revolt. In this film the adolescent protagonist is a cross-country runner who refuses a sure victory so as to deny spreading any glory to the institution – a reform school – that both sponsors and exploits him. In the short story, it was the Borstal's potbellied governor at whom the loss was directed; but the lads caught on faster than most that the race was lost on purpose, for them.

In *The Art of the Motor*, Paul Virilio makes a significant point about athletic training: "we notice that the goal of training is synchronization of movement to the detriment of diachronization. It is now a matter of severely limiting *time for conscious intervention* on the part of the subject, to the point where the body seems to act of its own accord, without the aid of reflection, oblivious to the present world and so freed from doubt and hestitation."[2] Don't think – get into the game, the rhythm, the pace. Switch off because reflection slows one down; doubt is, in short, a drag. As is ambivalence, even if it erupts from the unconscious, for it ruins everyone else's plans. And this is the charm of ambivalence for it brings out an undisciplinable element in the athlete. Of course, sporting narratives have special places reserved for losers: agony and suffering are easily spectacularized. There is even a sub-genre of sports videos devoted to errors recuperable as comic events known to aficionados as "bloopers." But this strips them of ambivalence and radicality. Only a radical loser snatches defeat from the jaws of victory, while the ordinary loser ends up in the hospital or wearing the corporate badges of ignominious victory.

Virilio's reading of the need to overcome the temptation of reflection is perfectly suited to the dash, but it cannot be generalized; nor does it apply unequivocally to short, fast races. The fastest human runs the shortest race, to be sure, in which there is no time for even a backwards glance. Ben Johnson's infamous backwards glance at Carl Lewis at the Seoul Olympics was evidence enough that something monumental had taken place; an extraordinary moment of observation had entered the race before its finish. Johnson's eruption of reflection was simultaneously displaced into a racist representation in which thinking was denied to him in advance: paradoxically, the more he affirmed his unthinking, his innocence about his pharmaceutical regime, the more he was animalized and machinized (the animalization of black athletes was much in evidence in the television advertising for the Atlanta Olympics on CBC in which Canadian sprinter Donovan Bailey was placed in a line

61

of luxury mammals – horses – with a "blood line" traceable to Jesse Owens; indeed, the ridiculous stunt in Charlottetown in 1998 during which Johnson raced a horse and a stock car fits into this racist bestiary of animals of burden). Yet, any further indication of reflection on Johnson's part would have called into question, for the vultures capitalizing on his plight, his lack of obedience, his betrayal of the sport and the Olympic spirit, his humiliation of the country, and his abandonment of the children who idolized him. All of this was foreshadowed in the brief instant of the race when he looked back: the gesture through whose appearance he became a winner who could not win or a winner who won too decisively. A winner, in other words, who thought too much.

Roland Barthes, commenting on cycling, picks up on this theme in the following way. In Barthes' mythology of the Tour de France bicycle race, the division of labour in a cycling team requires a strategic meditative role in which one racer takes the "cerebral burden upon himself."[3] Even here, Barthes observes, it is possible for a racer to think too much. When this happens the racer becomes a winner rather than a player. Winning can be tarnished by too much thought.

Ultimately, Johnson was not permitted to be an ordinary loser in the commonplace gamble of doping. This is not new. At least since Tommie Smith and John Carlos raised their gloved fists in black power salutes on the podium after the 200 metre dash at the 1968 Olympics in Mexico City, struggles against injustice, especially when they are expressed in powerful gestures accompanying winning performances, put everything at stake. The first thing to disappear is one's athletic career. This is the context in which Johnson's backward glance needs to be placed. Johnson's gesture was not expressly political, rather, it was excessively athletic. An eruption all the same, but not a radical one. Johnson was not a radical loser in the Baudrillardian sense. Instead, only his gesture of looking behind him was excessive: his reflection was as much his undoing as his dope.[4]

Notes

1. The key texts are Baudrillard's essay "Concerning the Fulfillment of Desire in Exchange Value," *For a Critique of the Political Economy of the Sign*, Charles Levin (trans.), St. Louis: Telos Press, 1981, pp. 204-12 and Alan Sillitoe's *The Loneliness of the Long Distance Runner*, London: Pan, 1959. In general, the notion of loss belongs more to dissipation than to throwing a contest. Billiards is, of course, the "gay altar of dissipation," as

James Hall put it in his 1829 story, "The Billiard Table," which leads off Robert Byrne's collection *Great Pool Stories*, San Diego: Harcourt Brace, 1995. Pool stories are often moral tales of shipwrecked egos on a green island of felt, swaggering fat men, and stakes that spiral out of control as the night mysteriously slips away.

2. Paul Virilio, *The Art of the Motor*, Julie Rose (trans.), Minneapolis: University of Minnesota Press, 1995, p. 94.

3. Roland Barthes, "The Tour de France As Epic," in *The Eiffel Tower*, Richard Howard (trans.), New York: Hill and Wang, 1979, p. 86.

4. See Gamal Abdel-Shedid's "Running Clean: Ben Johnson and the Un-Making of Canada," *Borderlines* 46 (1998): 25-7 for an analysis of the racist "forgetful remembering" of Johnson in the Canadian imagination, especially in relation to the violations of Silken Laumann and Ross Rebagliati. A fascinating document of pseudo-subversion, and not at all veiled racism, appeared in a mock ad in *Frank* magazine (12 April 1995) in which Ben Johnson is made to exclaim: "Silken, You Bastard, Go Back to Finland."

VOLUNTARY SERVITUDE

In its

time during the late 1980s and early 90s, Jean Baudrillard's travelogue *America* was reviewed widely by every wannabe postmodernist. It garnered largely uncritical or, better, acritical acclaim. Unfortunately, I got into the act as well.[1] And I want to do it again but, this time, with a difference: I will revisit it as a sportswriter covering the cultural beat. This is strategy of reading against the grain that I often adopt: read theory as a sportswriter, or write sports as a theorist. Read and write against the grain of restrictive categories, run circles around hermeneuts desperate to nail down their interpretations, cross borders in an entirely undisciplined manner.

Baudrillard not only likes losers, but is fascinated by inconsequential performances of self-affirmation which are the very stuff of the sporting life. His book is littered with references to breakdancing, the New York Marathon, jogging, and body building. Baudrillard's scattered remarks are organized around two themes: death and narcissism.

Baudrillard does not hold a grudge against the breakdancers he sees in New York, spinning around on their bits of cardboard. They perform "feat[s] of acrobatic gymnastics" even if they simultaneously appear to be digging holes for themselves, with themselves, like so many human back hoes. What is the goal of this grave digging? Baudrillard notes: "they seem to be digging a hole for themselves with their own bodies, from which to stare out in the ironic, indolent pose of the dead." It is the final pose of a routine that grabs Baudrillard's attention:

a sudden nonchalant pose with one elbow on the ground which reminds him of figures on Etruscan tombs. The pose is derisive, and it is a challenge of some sort rather than an invitation to get down. It is part of a collective as opposed to an individuated death; in other words, it is social and gestural rather than psychological and interior. Those witnessing the performance and pose of death with which it ends are therefore not alone before death, as they are before the embalmed corpses on display in funeral parlours. The pose is so obviously artificial that it doesn't pretend to give death a natural, fresh look. This pose of the dead has attitude, and this is what Baudrillard appreciates.

He experiences precisely the opposite before the spectacle of the New York Marathon. A mass of 17,000 people running alone, seeking death by exhaustion. Crossing the finish line affords the runner nothing more than the international symbol, as Baudrillard puts it, of voluntary servitude: I DID IT! Before Just Do It! there was this announcement of profoundly futile accomplishment, of a feat without consequence. Baudrillard calls this run to the death a form of "demonstrative suicide." No message of collective victory. Just the advertisement of an existence, like graffiti tags. There is nothing more in reserve or to do after you have been all that you can be.

Baudrillard loves New York. He is echoing the words of Jean-Paul Sartre from the mid-1940s, and the cheesy slogan of the 1970s – *J'aime New York* – a simple, empty loyalty. I did it and I love it. It's all the same to Baudrillard because New York is a place for autistic performances.

But the west coast has its own version of voluntary athletic servitude: jogging. "Narcissistic refraction" rules the Baudrillardian world of sports: breakdancing, body building, jogging with a walkman, word processing. The same "blank solitude" before the computer screen, the mirrors in the gym, the headphones. Baudrillard calls this a "frantic self-referentiality" reminiscent of the privations undergone by the fathers of the desert, the third-century Stylites who sat atop pillars. It is as far beyond narcissism as metaphysics is beyond physics. I am the loop; I am hooked up to myself; I am into myself. "This 'into' is the key to everything," Baudrillard admits, whether it's one's own body or ideas. It used to be that one could be into something other than oneself. This, he suggests, is no longer the case.

Jogging is the worst. Joggers are leisurely suicides, "protagonists of an easy-does-it Apocalypse." Running alone up and down the mist-shrouded beach in Santa Barbara, oblivious to their surroundings, in a groove toward the "ecstasy of fatigue," the joggers move straight ahead in the production of self-destruction. This is a new form of self-indulgence. They are the shadows of Baudrillard's postmodern America, on the lam from Plato's cave, religious shrouds, the atomic bomb, and undoubtedly from Baudrillard himself, yet another French professor on vacation in America.

Notes
1. "Adventures in the Dromosphere," *Borderlines* 17 (1989-90): 34-6.

OLYMPIAN CUTENESS

I am

haunted by cuteness. It has become strange to me, stripped of childhood affection. The
calculation of cuteness is nowhere more evident than in the commodities of children's culture,
marked by age and gender lines that work themselves out in the division between invincible,
violent or whimsical, cuddly figures. But what really makes cuteness a compelling topic for
me is that children themselves are, in certain contexts, being turned out – which includes
their social identities, body types, etc. – in terms of cuteness. I am writing before the television screen and the spectacle of the summer Olympics (1996). Women's gymnastics has
broken through the clutter of terminal reportage. I have also just finished reading Joan Ryan's
Little Girls in Pretty Boxes: The Making and Breaking of Elite Gymnasts and Figure Skaters,[1] in
which she outlines how the bodies and psyches of elite athletes are shaped and broken by
their coaches and parents. Cuteness is not only a form of Disneyesque "imagineering." It is a
regime that has been violently imposed upon the young women on the screen. This essay
begins and ends with cuteness in the Olympics, and in the middle I try to explain what
cuteness means and why it is an Olympian affair.

Walt Disney is said to have pinned a note over each of his animators' desks reminding
them to "Keep it cute!" Walt's word was, as we know, heeded to the letter and the figure. Not
all cuteness is so Mickey Mouse. The cultivation of cuteness is not restricted to the cartoon

bestiary, despite the remarkable array of cute mice and other rodents – made in Disneyland or elsewhere – found there.

Mickey was not always so cute. As he evolved, if you will, he became progressively more juvenile in appearance. This common tendency to render animals in juvenile form, despite their actual maturity, is known as neoteny. The circles that gave form to Mickey's body – especially his ears which very early on ceased to be drawn in perspective – were subtly adjusted to signify that his mean streak and off-colour hijinks from his "Steamboat Willie" days had been cut short: no more stripping and spanking frankfurters or hoisting Minnie by the knickers. Mickey's progressive juvenilization moved toward the features of his young nephew Morty. This was accomplished by an increase in eye size, head length and cranial vault size; Mickey's arms and legs and snout were thickened, his legs jointed, and his ears were moved back. He became progressively cute.

A similar phenomenon has occurred in women's gymnastics since the 1970s. In her provocative book on elite gymnastic training and culture as a form of child abuse, Ryan reminds us that, today, "once the athletes become women, their elite careers wither." Figures from 1976 and 1992 reveal that US Olympic women gymnasts have become on average only a year younger, but six and half inches shorter, and 23 pounds lighter. It needs to be kept in mind that the American team was, already in the 1970s, horribly out of step with international developments in women's gymnastics and the emergence of Olympic gold medalists Olga Korbut in 1972 (four feet eleven inches, 85 pounds) and Nadia Comaneci in 1976 (five feet tall, 85 pounds). Elite women's gymnastics has become the domain of what most reporters like to call "pixies," but without an element of mischief. The progressive juvenilization of women's bodies in elite gymnastics is what I would call a regime of cuteness parallel to Mickey Mouse's neotenization – not to mention the Disneyfication of the Olympics. But the issue here is not the cartoon bestiary. There are ample biomechanical reasons why only such small, light bodies can perform the routines demanded of them. These do not explain the influence of coaches such as Bela Karolyi – former coach of Comaneci who defected from Romania to the United States in 1981 and is credited with, among other things, almost single-handedly establishing the pixie model of gymnast – in shaping the aesthetic and technical ideal of successful gymnastic performances and the appearance of the athletes. US gymnasts in Atlanta had their hair pulled back into buns wrapped with ribbons and sprinkled with sparkle dust, their faces carefully made up, smiles-on-demand and gestures practiced for the cameras and judges, while their coach, Karolyi, played cheerleader from the stands before the partisan crowd and Martha Karolyi hugged the girls as they left the floor after their performances.

There are only two Olympic events in which make-up is part of the equipment: women's gymnastics and synchronized swimming. Ryan herself raises the issue of cuteness as a kind of dissuasive quality akin to fetishism: despite what she views as putative child abuse, "there is little outcry about gymnastics, perhaps because the sport's amateur status suggests that the athletes are competing for fun. And perhaps because the girls seem so *cute* .... Gymnasts ... are 'acceptable' female athletes who are brave but not macho, muscled but not bulky, competitive but still vulnerable." In this respect cuteness is a great neutralizer – of size, strength, sexuality, aggression, complexity, individuality, and even change.

What, exactly, is cuteness?

In the eighteenth century, the term *cute* was shortened from *acute*, and assumed the sense of sharpness as in keen-witted and shrewd. The loss of the accented vowel of *a*cute was eventually accompanied by the loss of the term's applicability to either gender; by the nineteenth century, it acquired gender specificity and was commonly used of women, suggesting feminine cunning. In the twentieth century, *cute* takes on further shades of meaning, particularly in American slang, where it is an adjective of approval; yet it may also be used of male athletes who are clever and cunning in their manoeuvres ("cute move"). Traditionally, a *cutie* is an attractive young woman. It is assumed the speaker is a heterosexual male. In the preppie lexicon, *completely cute* is used by young women to describe approvingly a potential male partner.

More generally, *cute* applies equally well to young women and men cross-speaking of one another and of other members of their own sexes, and to animals, children, and things of all kinds; indeed, parts of bodies may be positively appraised with the adjectival use of cute, as in "cute tush."

Cute also signifies beings or objects whose attributes elicit affective responses. The attributes of cuteness produce a feeling of warmth and closeness accompanied by behaviour patterns of caring associated with brood-tending. What are these attributes? In the early

1940s Austrian ethologist Konrad Lonrenz developed his *Kindchenschema*, the infant schema for the aesthetic proportions of the heads of human and non-human animals considered to be cute. His research provides a list of the physical (as well as one behavioural) attributes constituting an ethological definition of cuteness:

1. Head large and thick in proportion to the body;
2. Protruding forehead large in proportion to the size of the rest of the face;
3. Large eyes below the middle line of the total head;
4. Short, stubby limbs with pudgy feet and hands;
5. Rounded, fat body shape;
6. Soft, elastic body surfaces;
7. Round, chubby cheeks;
8. Clumsiness

Lorenz describes an innate releasing mechanism (IRM) in human adults that is triggered by configurations of key attributes, in this case those of cute infants, eliciting affective patterns of behaviour such as the desire to cuddle, pat, embrace, use pet names in a high-pitched voice, generally care for, perhaps nurse, bend down one's head towards, etc. IRMs react positively to the sum of heterogeneous attributes, defined not in terms of absolute values but, rather, by the perception of intervals and relations between attributes. Lest one assume that the IRM is thoroughly innate or a drive, Lorenz defines it as a function that may be made more selective by learning and given direction and specification by culture-specific practices.

Importantly, IRMs may be activated more effectively by simulated models than by natural beings. The attributes of cuteness are, then, vehicular, since they travel well from one species to another. Responses are remarkably unreflective when faced with supernormal objects consisting of qualitatively and quantitatively modified attributes. There are limits to such modifications, after which cute becomes eerie. Many filmic creatures occupy a threshold between cute and eerie, as one may recall in the case of E.T., some of whose attributes (protruding forehead, head size, and large eyes) were conventionally cute while many others were not (gangly limbs, long fingers, wrinkled skin). Ethologists often borrow examples from the doll and fashion industries to refine and extend their findings. In the 1940s, Lorenz talked about the Kewpie doll as a liminal figure between cute and eerie. Examples of Disney cartoon animals and kitsch art abound in ethology to illustrate the overemphasis of baby characteristics in cute representations, adding that certain breeds of dogs such as the Pekinese have been bred to be perfect substitutes for the unfulfilled desire of mothering in the aged.

Even the most sophisticated appeals to "nature cute" through pudgy paws and chubby cheeks must reckon with the ease with which such attributes are exploited commercially. To feel that beings or objects are engaging, sweet and appealing may entail a pathological involvement in interpersonal relations marked by an unwelcomed intrusiveness, the violation of bodily integrity and social space and, in short, harassment. The biological argument makes the attributes of cuteness a kind of standing invitation to touch, embrace and fawn over, even if the cutie in question is a person with no interest in this sort of thing. Ethologists are not much interested in ethics.

Kitsch may exploit cuteness for commercial purposes, but the commercial exploitation of cuteness and sentimentality in general is a matter of serious concern for what is called the industry for social expression. Cuteness circulates around interpersonal relations in many people's everyday lives in the form of greeting cards. Critical readings of the history and social meaning of the greeting card vary enormously depending on the position taken on the industry leader Hallmark Cards Inc., and the degree to which the pre-fabricated messages of such cards are considered to constitute genuine or simulated expressions of a wide range of feelings appropriate to an equally diverse range of social and familial situations.

A visit to any of Hallmark's retail boutiques provides evidence of the robust culture of cuteness and its micro-encodings in the cultural properties that define the product range available in a given local market and cultural context. This teaching or training may be a corporate invasion of everyday life, but it also reveals the range of combinatorial possibilities presented by the attributes of cuteness in the manufacture of product lines carrying market-tested constructions of recognizable creatures and pseudo-species of all sorts.

Not all of the ethological attributes of cuteness are present in elite women gymnasts. Clumsiness pertains better to newborns and not at all to gymnasts. The appearance of clumsiness, which results from stubby limbs, is one of the features of paradigmatically cute, that is, easily anthropomorphized, animals such as Panda bears. Elasticity is a key attribute, as is shortness and smallness in general. Chubbiness is ruled out, although rigorous training cannot completely erase round cheeks. Indeed, the faces of girls are much flatter than those of infants, and their features have left their roundness behind. Cosmetics help to enhance certain key features such as the eyes and cheeks, whose size, roundness and visibility at a distance approach cute dimensions but are no match, of course, for the exaggerations of cartoon characters such as the uniformed school girls of *Sailor Moon*, whose eyes are alarmingly large. In a supremely redundant but emotionally resonant way, *cute* is often used together with *little* as in a description of the pixie gymnasts having "cute little haircuts." It is difficult, then, to pin down with any precision the exact thing that makes these gymnasts cute. For like the ethological definition of cuteness, Olympian cuteness depends on the interdependent relations of several attributes, the maintenance of which requires the prolongation of immaturity resistant to puberty (i.e., the bodies of these gymnasts are lean and their clean lines would be interrupted by breasts and hips which, together with a change in bone density, weight gain, shape change, and overall flexibility, would make the execution of the most demanding manoeuvres difficult if not impossible). This construction of cuteness gathers together a range of terms, such as princess, sprite, and pixie, which simultaneously point to the supernatural ideal upon which women gymnasts are judged – and some seem to approach while in full flight – and the complex codes of submissiveness, not only to the will and whim of coaches, to the team, to training and the Olympic dream, but in the suspension of the passage from dependency to independence, from girlhood to adulthood.

Cuteness, in short, is cultivated for its vulgar aesthetic and emotional delights in an entirely patronizing manner. To call a young female gymnast cute is to relieve oneself of the responsibility of understanding what it is to be an elite athlete. The point of Ryan's investigative journalism was to draw back the curtain on elite sports training for women. As soon as it is no longer possible to neotenize a young woman in the sport of elite gymnastics, she may be discarded. It is, after all, maturation that the regime of cuteness tries to forestall. Neoteny is not a Mickey Mouse affair when the regime of cuteness requires punishing physical, pharmaceutical, and psychological methods to keep puberty at bay.

Gymnastics

Notes

1. Joan Ryan, *Little Girls in Pretty Boxes: The Making and Breaking of Elite Gymnasts and Figure Skaters*, New York: Times-Warner, 1996. This book is based on Ryan's articles for the *San Francisco Examiner* and her work was counted among the best sports writing in 1995 by Dan Jenkins and Glenn Stout, editors of the 1995 edition of the Houghton-Mifflin annual publication (since 1991) *The Best American Sports Writing*.

DISPATCHED

Sport has

commonly fired the science fictional imagination in the direction of cruel spectacles such as "rollerball." Technologically enhanced speeds, hurtling, machined objects, and edges with surgical sharpness make death and dismemberment the stakes of matches between players who are essentially advanced cyborgs with a wrestler's sense of showmanship. A particularly good example of the two themes of machined projectiles and death appear in a long-forgotten collection of science fiction short stories arranged around sporting themes, *Arena: Sports SF*, edited by Ed Ferman and Barry Malzberg.[1] In "Mirror of Ice," Gary Wright stretches out and dramatizes a bobsled course, increases the speed of the one-man sled (imagine a missile-like luge), and adds the element of multiple sleds racing for the finish line and a rich purse in a study of what may be the final race of a champion in his enclosed cockpit on skis, snug in a G-suit, awaiting death like so many other racers around whose fatal accidents the tradition of this sport has formed. Forget *Cool Runnings*, for this is a mutant bobsledding in a world without Disney: "*someone once, laughing, had said, 'Without peer, we are the world's fastest suicides'.*"

Bobsleds twisting down an ice chute may not be everyone's cup of tea. The standard science fictional announcement of an inevitable metallic KO does not diminish the themes of finely tuned and turned machines and death. They are not trapped in science fictional worlds.

Rather, they render the drama of the city streets and the weight and speed differences of bicycles and motorized vehicles. Bike messengers inhabit a science fiction become real: the ground zero of soft flesh exposed to heavy traffic that is not to be confused with the unmediated pleasure of accidents exposed in David Cronenberg's *Crash*. The fantastic objects of science fictional sports do not need to be reinvented in this contemporary scenario. The road simply puts them into everyday forms as cars and buses bearing down with the intensity of hot metal on a messenger with whom they are supposedly sharing a lane. Anyone who has ever cycled in the city knows that motorized vehicles do not like to share. It is, then, for good reason that the zine of the San Francisco Bike Messenger Association, *Mercury Rising*, takes as its motto the ancient adage: "Don't kill the messenger."

Admittedly, I have moved rather quickly from science fiction to the city street by means of two themes. Now I want to pull back to science fiction – not to abandon bike messengers – but to find them again in a new way. This darting and dashing between science fiction and everyday traffic is my way of reading bike messenger association magazines. What I find most remarkable about messenger culture is that, as a death sport, if it is a sport at all, it not only pays respect to its fallen riders, but squarely faces the violence of the street and the death it delivers. The zines I have examined are records of sport, of the results of the latest cycle messenger championships, for example, and the results of street hassles and violence, as well as responses to them (both individual and collective, as in the Critical Mass protest rides, born in San Francisco, in which, on the last Friday of every month cyclists reclaim downtown streets, bringing traffic to a halt). In Toronto, Critical Mass has featured a ride through the Eaton Centre and protest tactics reminiscent of the yippies showering Santa Claus with Big Nothing Day dollar bills and pamphlets; this event is truly remarkable and entirely laudable. (And spreading – one summer night in Sydney, Australia, I stumbled onto a Critical Mass ride in the Glebe). Perhaps the obituary is the stylistic model of messenger writing. Although there are many people who think that messengering is a sport, it is surely postmodern since it erases divisions between work and play, lacks a facility proper in which it is performed, and doesn't play by the rules of the road – accounting for a large part of its charm and challenge. Bike messengers have even been demonized in television advertisements for the sake of four-wheel drive-consuming yuppie families who have fled in fear to the 'burbs from the rough terrain of the downtown streets.[2]

75

In cyberpunk writing, the worlds evoked are nearly our own, right down to the hyperrealized codes of an info-environment and its proliferating subcultures. Post-millennial urban life consists of transits between privatized and derelict public spaces. In *Virtual Light*, William Gibson negotiates these transits, set largely in San Francisco, through the predicaments of bike messengers. The city is science fictional and real, and it makes you wonder about a tomorrow that has all the trappings of today. There are many reasons for this, one of which is Gibson's acknowledged debt to *Mercury Rising*, one of whose editors, Fur, provided a complete set of back issues.[3] Cycle messenger culture provides Gibson with two characters, Chevette Washington and Samuel Saladin DuPree (Sammy Sal), both riding for Allied Messenger Services. While admiring, with some horror, the photograph of an amphalang in a shop in the Haight, Chevette meets Sammy Sal, who endorses this augmentation. She notices him the following day in Union Square "hanging with a bunch of bike messengers." His gear and wheels are impressive, and Gibson enters wholeheartedly into the minutiae of Chevette's technological and cultural fascination with the styles of the messengers and their fictionalized bikes: glowing, pulsing rims, internal sound systems, and locks that seal with a thumbprint. Gibson's ingenious description of Chevette's anti-theft system on the ultra-light paper bike she acquires when she becomes a messenger with the help of Sammy Sal – the sprayed-on rust and frayed duct tape, the cheap Radio Shack voice alarms, and the electrical shock her bike is capable of delivering as well – transfigures the mundane concerns of messengers. Who, after all, hasn't had a bike stolen? Who needs a bike more than a messenger? What desperate inventor hasn't dreamed, after reading Gibson's book, of tinkering with batteries, cables and the like with the goal of actually building the sort of bike alarm with the capacity to fry the genitals of a would-be thief? Ah, sweet sadistic dreamers like these really do love their bicycles.[4]

Back to the street. In the August 1995 issue of *Mercury Rising*, six pages are devoted in memoriam to Thomas Meredith, who died as a result of injuries sustained when he was run over by a San Francisco MUNI bus in September, 1994. In San Francisco, the city's MUNI buses are waging an unspoken war with cycle messengers, while in Toronto the enemy appears in the form of taxi cabs. In a moving eulogy his sister, America Meredith, a co-founder of *Mercury Rising*, provides a biographical overview and details of the wake and burial. The death ceremonials of messenger culture are described in these terms: "The next day, messengers blocked Montgomery Street and 15 people were arrested. For weeks flowers were laid at the accident site. Thomas' death was all over the news – most of the information was distorted or concocted. About 150 people showed up at the wake at South Park, which continued to Mission Rock in messenger tradition, where my mother and I threw a bike basket filled with flowers into the bay .... Critical Mass was dedicated to his memory and had 1, 200 participants." In the October 1995 issue, an obituary on the back cover acknowledges the death of Dan Lutge, not as a result of an accident, but from "big poisons." Again, the collective memory of the community is acute: "Many people knew the legend – his diapers changed on a dispatch table, the awesome record of 122 tags in one day, and now, barely 30, gone." Ceremony, history, individuals of mythic proportions: these are the elements of a sub-culture irreducible to the vagaries of fashion. The staggering simplicity and beauty of a bike basket, filled with flowers, being dropped into the ocean shatters in a single stroke the melancholy of the funeral wreath and sterile enclosures of mainstream dealings with the dead, monopolized by funeral directors, the clergy and the coroner.

On the web site of Toronto's organ of the messenger community, *Hideous White Noise*, Be Smiley's "Conversations from the Summer of 1996" remembers the deaths of four cyclists in the city during the past year. Smiley is an artist "who is having a hard time 'getting the concept' of using a one-and-a-half ton vehicle to haul around a cell phone and a box of Kleenex." This obituary of sorts reaches beyond the messenger community to expose the prone position of cycling in the blind spots of trucks and cars. Ghoulishness is also on the agenda in The Crusty Old Guy's "Hellowe'en, Toronto Style" report on the outlaw bike race that featured thirteen checkpoints (which could be visited in any order, and at which baseball cards were hidden) in churches, graveyards, war and dead pet memorials and, perhaps most appropriately, the coroner's office. If the danger of messenger work was ever in doubt, further evidence is provided by its sixth place ranking in a list of the most dangerous professions in Pelton and Aral's *Most Dangerous Places*. Indeed, arrests and injuries resulting from recent Critical Mass rides are exposed in all their legal gory!

Beyond morbid fascination and the burgeoning crash culture of extreme performances; beside the legal and illegal rides of the Alley Cats with their – what else? – cigarette sponsor-

77

ship, somewhere a messenger is negotiating an exhaust-slicked road, making eye contact with the driver of a lurching vehicle whose destination is at best uncertain, like the weak member of a herd locked in the gaze of a predator. The truth of the fiction is this: Don't kill the messenger.

Notes

1. *Arena: Sports SF*, Edward L. Ferman and Barry N. Malzberg (eds.), Garden City: Doubleday, 1976.

2. Toronto currents in bike culture include such groups as C.U.N.T.: Chicks United for Non-Noxious Transportation. To mark the mega-city debate the CUNTs issued volume 5 (Spring 1997) of their zine on the theme of "You are now entering MEGA-CUNTRY," declaring their desire to redraw their own boundaries, build their grease monkey skills while curing sufferers of the nasty disorder Bike Repair Despair, and extolling the virtues of a pierced clitoral hood rubbing against a bicycle seat. Appropriately, the all-lesbian bike courier company in San Francisco goes by the name of Lickety-Split.

3. William Gibson, *Virtual Light*, New York: Random House, 1993. Gibson wrote: "I am indebted to Markus, aka Fur, one of the editors of *Mercury Rising*, published by and for the San Francisco Bike Messenger Association, who kindly provided a complete file of back issues." Fur died of an apparent drug overdose in San Francisco in 1997.

4. In his description of Cloud Gardens, an urban park in the financial district of downtown Toronto, Charles Mandel notes: "With its angled surfaces, bridges and a raised amphitheatre that doubles as a convenient bike jump, it has become an impromptu stage for couriers to show off to their peers a few stunts between parcel drops" ("Soothing the Urban Soul," *Canadian Geographic* May/June 1998).

HOCKEY AND CULTURE

From the

mainstream to the avant-garde, hockey has served as an all-terrain vehicle for the aesthetic explorations of English and French Canadians. Whether it is Roch Carrier's famous short story "Une abominable feuille d'érable sur la glace" (the banal translation of which, "The Hockey Sweater," loses the anti-Maple Leafs message), or Serge Morin and Serge Dufaux's 1983 film *De l'autre côté de la glace* (a still from this film featuring a whimsical goaltender appeared on the cover of the art magazine *Parallélogramme* 19/4, 1994), cultural and political allegiances have been registered through hockey's potent symbols. Indeed, for a poignant and sporting expression of Québécois nationalism, one need look no further than Rick Salutin's play of 1977, *Les Canadiens*, in which the election of the Parti Québécois on November 15, 1976 lifts the burden of political expression from the backs of the players onto those of the Péquistes. Still, I want to break apart this Canadian binarism, without diminishing the importance of artistic accomplishments based upon it, and in so doing let all the hockey being played across the country and beyond the rink engage a broader understanding of the subjectivities, cultures, and rituals of the game, with tolerance and respect. Discussions of hockey all too often suffer from normopathic tendencies that both assume standard or normative definitions of how to participate, in some measure, in its manifestations, and a pathological attachment to such norms that crush plurality and all creative combinations and applications of the game in the expanded field of culture.

WHAT IS THE PLURAL OF HOCKEY?

When the

New York weekly *The Village Voice* (March 9, 1993) ran excerpts from the libretto of Torontonian Brad Walton's hockey opera *The Loves of Wayne Gretzky*, in which the author stages an affair between the Great One and the Pittsburgh Penguin's star Mario Lemieux, the routine subjective formations (masculine, white, nationalistic) that have typified hockey culture were affectively queered. Gay hockey opera may be a fleeting genre, but its implications for making the hockey subject aware of his or her homoerotic investments in the game is substantial. This fictional episode led to further coverage in the *Voice* (August 16, 1994) of Daniel Gawthrop's articles in *Xtra West* and the *Vancouver Sun* extolling the virtues of ex-Vancouver Canuck star Pavel Bure: "androgynous, fawn-like features ... lips like rose petals, bedroom eyes and fashionably coiffed hair." Coverage of hockey fans in Canadian gay communities, in the *Globe & Mail* and by CBC commentator Don Cherry – whose televisual performances during intermission are tied to shifting constructions of hockey consumers, enabling him to refer, out of one side of his mouth, to foreign players as "sissies," and out of the other side, to welcome gay fans into the fold – during a *Hockey Night in Canada* broadcast brought the issue of the diverse constituencies of hockey to the fore and further invested the game with a remarkable pluralism.

If one were to look for these kind of openings to new, plural hockey subjectivities in recent books such as Richard Gruneau and David Whitson, *Hockey Night In Canada: Sport, Identities, and Cultural Politics*,[1] one would only be disappointed. The tired, singular, hetero-sexual, hockey masculinity, and in certain important instances, the breakthroughs, and how they are not so subtly devalued, of young women such as goaltender Manon Rheaume at the professional level, are rehearsed by social scientists Gruneau and Whitson. While the authors are better prepared, in methodological terms, to understand labour issues, they lack the expertise to speak convincingly of culture and identity. A few references to cultural theory appear here and there in the text, but they only enable Gruneau and Whitson to conclude that hockey is part of a global, postmodern, capitalist culture, even though it offers "new spaces for identity formation" to so-called new groups, about whom they have nothing to say and, clearly, from their tenured cocoons, are unlikely to learn anything about.

Notes

1. Richard Gruneau and David Whitson, *Hockey Night in Canada: Sport, Identities, and Cultural Politics*, Toronto: Garamond, 1993. I published a review of this book under the title of "What is the Plural of Hockey?" *Fuse* 18/4 (1995): 46-7.

HOCKEY NIGHT ON THE REZ

Tomson Highway

understands well the strange effects a hockey game can have on a community. In his play, *Dry Lips Oughta Move to Kapuskasing*,[1] the fictional reserve of Wasaychigan Hill experiences a revolution when, in Zachary Jeremiah Keechigeesik's dream, the women of the reserve form a hockey team called the Wasy Wailerettes. The "particular puck" with which they eventually play circulates throughout the play, finding its way at one point into the bosom of Gazelle Nataways, only to be shaken loose later in the action, before the final game sequence (which is really a dream sequence) can unfold. The repetition of the question "Where's the puck?" heralds a nightmare sequence in which Nanabush (in this instance as the spirit of Black Lady Halked – a parody of the pseudo-native emblem of the Chicago Black Hawks) sits upon a "giant luminescent puck." At the opening of the play it was Nanabush (as the spirit of Gazelle Nataways) who, with a bump of her hip, turned on the television to Hockey Night in Canada. Later, when Zachary awakes from his dream to return to the reality of his wife Hera and their new baby, he remarks how much the moon looked like a puck last night – harking back to the vision of Nanabush, and asks his wife whether she has ever thought of playing hockey, to which she replies: "Yea right. That's all I need is a flying puck right in the left tit, neee." With the hockey game long over and The Smurfs on the television screen before him, all Zachary can do is point out that Smurfs don't play hockey!

You won't find Tomson Highway in Gruneau and Whitson's *Hockey Night in Canada*. And you won't hear about Maple Leaf great George Armstrong, whose mother was part Ojibway and French Canadian, who was subjected to the kind of racism that almost every hockey writer covering the "original six" – not Nations, but NHL teams – considered inevitable: he was nicknamed Chief. It is through caricatured and stereotyped nicknames, emblems, mascots, and marketing reductions of all kinds that real cultural differences and traditions are rendered benign and slightly ridiculous for those who unthinkingly consume them, primarily children. Racist stereotypes are the currency of the dominant hockey discourse, and they are also commodities, the exchange of which fosters belonging, as in "my team." The cultural identity created by them is impoverished because it is fundamentally defined by the marketplace and irredeemably racist.

Gruneau and Whitson confess that they grew up in the 1950s and 1960s in Toronto. They do not tell us if they remember Armstrong's nickname, nor what it meant for them to have the name of Tim Horton loosen itself from hockey and become just another donut shop (well, not just another shop since Eddie Shack opened his donut shop in Caledon, northwest of Toronto, thereby expanding the well-established cultural bond between donuts and cops into the hockey realm). A further, more general bond needs to be investigated: what I call fast ice, fast food. The investments of hockey players, both during their athletic careers and upon retirement, have pointed toward fast food outlets: Does anyone remember Bobby Orr pizza? How about John Anderson burgers? I've already mentioned donuts. What do you think they serve at Gretzky's? And the food at Don Cherry's Grapevine! Round, tepid, greasy foods, sitting in pools of fat, like pucks on melting ice. Anyway, Gruneau and Whitson meticulously avoid analyses of specific products. Remarkably, they even avoid the important matter of collecting in hockey circles.

Gruneau and Whitson claim that "'communities' formed around acts of consumption … are not political communities in any meaningful sense of the word." One can agree that capitalist subjectivity requires reductions and limitations and still understand that the pursuit of hockey through consumption needs to be freed from spectatorship and the caps-and-shirts analyses in order to move into areas of "social identification" that are less obvious but no less political. The very notions of social and public and community have rendered identification problematic. The paths of subject formation and identification are tangled up in donuts and memories and the fictional fact that Dry Lips oughta move to the Kap because she fell down, blocking the slap shot of her teammate Hera Keechigeesik, and denying her a sure goal.

Notes
1. Tomson Highway, *Dry Lips Oughta Move To Kapuskasing*, Saskatoon: Fifth House, 1989.

HEROES AT THE BAR

Labour conflict

in sports inevitably leaves sportscasters and reporters in the difficult position of making the transition to the labour and even legal beats. This is an awkward situation at the best of times, as their airtime and word quotas prove to be difficult to fill with anything other than platitudes about the history and future of the game, the fans, the nation, and themselves (the latter is more important than one might think since the expression of indignation about labour strife is a sub-genre unto itself in sports reporting which provides the occasion for the lazy reporter to sound off). The issue is one of competence for the sportswriter. The boundaries of sports issues are confused by labour and legal complications. The point is that labour issues are perceived by many covering sports to intrude upon the sporting domain like unwelcome visitors, interlopers, as it were, trespassing upon well-marked home turf. After the comically short jail sentence given influential hockey player agent Alan Eagleson for fraud and embezzlement, there was a deafening silence concerning the legal victory of retired hockey players with regard to a pension fund surplus to which they had been denied access. Long-retired stars who are still household names and many also-rans subsist on tiny pensions and in some cases operate small businesses, like the very visible Eddie Shack, who has graduated from selling Christmas trees to donuts.

The main issue concerns the judicial interpretation of a technical legal contract, specifically, a pension plan. A further issue involved the question of when a trustee could be removed from his or her position. Law has, of course, its own codes about which sports reporters are often not competent to comment; perhaps even better, such competency would ruin their carefully cultivated personae.

Inflation in the early and mid-eighties gave rise to huge surpluses in the National Hockey League pension plan. This situation was not unique to hockey pensions. These surpluses arose for nurses, factory workers and others, and were unforeseen when such pension plans were established. Approximately $21 million of the league's pension surplus was directed by the board of the National Hockey League Pension Society toward the league to support collective bargaining agreements, and to provide a "holiday" from pension contributions (in the pension/insurance industry "surpluses" arise from "experience rate credits" – which are like cash as they can purchase "holidays" from contributions for employers, and additional pension benefits for employees). Some cash was also given to the six original clubs. Seven players challenged the allotment of funds, arguing that, according to the pension plan, any excess generated by the plan had to be applied *exclusively* for the benefit of player participants. They also challenged the ability of the pension society (due to earlier agreements, there were no longer any player representatives on its board) to continue as trustee.

At trial, the judge found that the original language of the 1947 pension plan and its regulations, as well as agreements and memorandums between the league and the players throughout the 1960s and 1970s, required that "all monies" and "any benefits" be held "for the benefit of the Participant exclusively." The pension society was not free to assign the excesses to the benefit of the league. The trial judge did not remove the pension society as trustee: its direction of funds was based on legal and actuarial advice that appeared sound.

The National Hockey League Pension Society appealed the part of the trial decision that required it to pay the surplus back into the pension fund. The players appealed the part of the decision that allowed the pension society to remain as trustee. The Ontario Court of Appeal upheld the decision of the trial judge on both the surplus issue and the trustee issue. Finally, the Supreme Court of Canada refused to grant leave to appeal to the pension society on July 28, 1994. The player participants are owed their additional benefits, including costs and pre- and post-judgment interest on $21 million.

For lawyers, this case is about reading the language of pension agreements, and will be used to support the claims of both employees and employers to pension surpluses. If sportscasters were able to comment on the legal matters influencing the business of gaming, hockey fans would be able to appreciate this case as a reward to retired players who worked for so little, and that the league went all the way to the Supreme Court trying to do these players out of a decent pension.

Perhaps this scenario will make it to the stage like John P. Moore's *The Lindros Trial: Extracts from Regina v. Eric Bryan Lindros*, the text of which was culled from the transcripts of the trial concerning an alleged incident in which the superstar spit beer at a woman in a Whitby, Ontario nightclub called "Koo Koo Bananas." But this one won't be played for laughs.[1]

Notes

1. When highly touted young star-in-waiting Alexandre Daigle entered the league in 1993 with the fledgling Ottawa Senators, he responded to a question about how he compared with Eric Lindros with the undeniably perspicacious phrase: "I drink my beer." Daigle hasn't amounted to much on the ice, but his way with words remains inspirational. Ottawa, it seems, is a bottomless pit of hockey marginalia. If only Andrew Hunter, curator of "Up North" and "Convergence," two exhibitions bringing together the mysterious disappearances of painter Tom Thomson and Maple Leaf Bill Barilko, and the great goalie Terry Sawchuk and American abstract expressionist Jackson Pollock, was a specialist in Russian art, he could integrate Alexei Yashin and his problematic donation to the National Arts Centre into his personal mythology of painting and hockey.

MINOR HISTORY

The colour

barrier was finally broken in the National Hockey League in 1958. This was rather late compared with major league baseball, for example, into which Jackie Robinson had broken eleven years earlier in 1947. Hockey was, in fact, the last North American sport to have black athletes enter its ranks. In that year on January 18 leftwinger William "Willie" O'Ree took to the ice for the Boston Bruins. A native of Fredricton, O'Ree had played semi-pro hockey for the Québec Aces in 1956-7 before being called up by Boston general manager Lynn Patrick. He played only two games for the Bruins in 1958, scoring no points. He played again for the Bruins in the 1960-61 season, appearing in 43 games, totaling 14 points.

During the 1959-60 season, O'Ree was sent to Kingston to play for the Frontenacs, the Bruins' farm team in the Eastern Professional Hockey League. At the beginning of the season it was noted without any further comment in the local press that O'Ree, one of coach Cal Gardner's "veterans" on what was a not particularly successful team, "was the first Negro to play in the NHL." In 50 games O'Ree tallied a very respectable 46 points. Although Kingston's claim to be the birthplace of hockey is still hotly contested by Montréal, Kingston can claim for itself an important place in black hockey history, and not only in the case of the trailblazing O'Ree. A smart hockey historian might stir the pot a little by arguing that the Québec Senior Hockey League of the mid to late 1940s was richer in black hockey talent, citing the all-black forward line (Manny McIntyre, and the Carnegie brothers, Herb and Ossie) iced by Sherbrooke in 1947 as evidence. That the brilliant playmaker and three-time MVP of the Québec league Herb Carnegie wasn't drafted is evidence, as sports reporter James Christie argued in the *Globe & Mail* (April, 1997), of the NHL's – specifically Conn Smythe's – backwardness and conservatism. It is also further evidence that the myth of the halcyon days of the original six needs to be finally debunked for the sake of a critical understanding of the game's history and reactionary politics.

O'Ree's career was mostly spent in the minors playing for Western Hockey League teams in Los Angeles and San Diego. Despite the obscurity that such a career path normally entails, he is widely known as "the Jackie Robinson of hockey" and has received civic honours from San Diego, honouring him as the first black player in the NHL, and recognition of his historic role from the New Brunswick Sports Hall of Fame in his hometown of Fredricton. Additionally, the NHL's Diversity Task Force sponsored a Willie O'Ree All-Star Weekend, bringing disadvantaged youths from the Chicago area to the game, when it was played there in 1991, to meet the players and develop their skills. 1998 was the fortieth anniversary of O'Ree's breakthrough. With the impetus of the fiftieth anniversary of Jackie Robinson's accomplishment being celebrated the year before, O'Ree's story garnered heavy but short-lived sports media attention. The moment, however, has passed.

89

Black hockey history has a further Kingston connection since another leftwinger, Tony McKegney, arguably the most successful black forward in the NHL to date, played OHA Junior A hockey for several seasons with the Kingston Canadians from 1974-75 through 1977-78, before he was drafted by the Buffalo Sabres. He was captain of the Canadians and scored prolifically as a junior.

McKegney was exposed to the virulent racism of the Old South when John Bassett drafted him in 1977 for the World Hockey Association's Birmingham Bulls. The threats by Bulls' season tickets holders to cancel their subscriptions if the team iced a black player convinced Bassett to release McKegney outright from his contract. McKegney's signing and release took place in less than a week's time. McKegney was not the first black player signed by a WHA team. Already in 1972 Alton White had played for the New York Raiders, making him the first black player in the league, followed closely by Bill Riley and Mike Marson of the Washington Capitals, who played together in 1974. McKegney's experience in

Kingston had certainly not prepared him for the racism he encountered in Birmingham. As captain of the Canadians, his picture was regularly in the press and his hockey exploits were followed with intense interest.

I have not mentioned all of the black NHLers (think about goaltenders for a moment and who comes to mind: obviously, the first black goalie, Grant Fuhr, who broke in with Edmonton in 1981, and then, more obscurely, Eldon "Pokey" Reddick, who played for the Jets in Winnipeg for a season and a half in the late 1980s) but the list is quite short. The more general point is that the telling of hockey history through its minoritarian elements expands the cultural field of the game and the potential for new subjective formations that are not limited by the standard accounts – either of the history of the game or the supposedly normal identities of those who play and watch it in the "great white north."

The celebration of O'Ree's accomplishment refocused the issue of telling minor histories onto the reporting of racist incidents on the ice in the NHL. In other words, racism is newsworthy, whether it is broken or practiced. The question was not: well, what about the history of aboriginal players? Rather, the focus of sports reporters and Canadian Press reports was on racist incidents between native and black players.[1]

The history of native Canadian players is revealing about the pathologically normal racism that has circulated for decades through the game. Even ephemera such as hockey cards contain patronizing cartoon images such as a line drawing of Reggie Leach, from the Berens River First Nation, with a feather and tomahawk from his rookie season with the California Golden Seals in 1972-73.

Notes

1. The entire question of racism in the NHL took off in November 1997 when Chris Simon, an Ojibway, publicly apologized for calling Mike Grier a "nigger." Soon after this event, Craig Berube was fined and suspended for calling Peter Worrell a "monkey." Mike Marson was interviewed in *The Toronto Star* the same month and described racist incidents during his years in the league in the 1970s. Editorial cartoons mocking the league's "sensitivity training" began to appear, and both Canadian Press and Associated Press continue to report incidents such as the episode between Chris Gratton and Peter Worrel in November 1998.

SOUL ON ICE

But this

is really a New York story. Even the most minor of histories can suffer from magisterial elements and normopathic tendencies, despite themselves. Here is a question: if O'Ree was first, who was second? This is where things become interesting.

In 1972 Team Canada beat the USSR in the eighth and final game to win the series four games to three. In the same year Harold Ballard was convicted of fraud and theft of money from the cashbox on Carlton, Maple Leaf Gardens. The Bruins won the cup. And, lest we forget, Nixon went to China. But 1972 was also the year that a rogue major hockey league got off the ground, the long defunct World Hockey Association (1972-1979). In the first year of its operation in 1972-73, the franchise in New York was called the Raiders. Originally, the owners wanted the team to play at the new arena in Naussau County on Long Island, but the NHL expanded onto the island at the same time and squeezed out the Raiders, sending them back, after an unsuccessful lawsuit, to Manhattan to negotiate with Madison Square Garden. During this period MSG was crying the blues to Mayor Lindsay about the heavy tax burden and threatening to relocate the Knicks basketball team, and the Rangers as well, to New Jersey if the city didn't give them a tax subsidy. The Raiders eventually found a home at MSG, although the high cost of tickets didn't help them.

In 1972 a hockey war had broken out between the NHL and WHA on numerous fronts, as players began to jump to the rogue league for hitherto unheard-of salaries. Acrimonious lawsuits filled the air. Well-known NHLers who had jumped to the new league such as Bobby Hull were not allowed to play for Team Canada. Some restraining orders on player mobility were successful, and others failed. In the midst of this legal circus the Raiders held a press conference on May 31st, 1972 to announce the signing of a new player.

The New York sporting press picked up the story and ran it the following day. The Raiders had announced the signing of Alton White, who would become the second black player to skate for a major league hockey team. May 31st was White's 27th birthday, and he met the press while cutting his birthday cake. This publicity stunt worked wonders. The Raiders managed to place a hockey story in the sports sections of New York papers in June during baseball season, just as Hank Aaron was catching Willie Mays on the all-time home run list! (Of course, today, with the NHL cup finals just getting underway in June, this feat does not appear noteworthy.) Organizationally, the Raiders were a mixed bag of talents: the general manager, Marvin Milkes, was a former basketball executive; in the fall of 1972, a Yankee baseball player signed a contract to provide colour commentary on local radio broadcasts of Raiders' games. They had a well respected coach, Camille Henry, but not much else going for them. In fact, by November, the franchise had collapsed financially, and was taken over by the league.

Alton White was not mentioned during the brief coverage of minor hockey history during the anniversary celebration of O'Ree's feats. His career was short and largely forgotten. When the Raiders hit the ice for the first time in October 1972 with White in the lineup, fourteen years had passed since O'Ree's breakthrough. At the time of White's signing, a few sportwriters noted that O'Ree was in fact still with the minor league San Diego team. O'Ree did not retire from hockey until 1980. At the time, then, two black players were active in professional hockey circles, neither in the NHL. And both were Maritimers (White was born in Amherst, Nova Scotia; he played junior hockey in Winnipeg with the Rangers from 1962-65 before moving to Fort Wayne in 1966, Columbus for three seasons, and onto Providence for one year before being drafted by New York). Fourteen years, in other words, hadn't made much of a difference for black players. The colour barrier, while technically broken, was still holding together.

Banal hockey wisdom has it that White's signing was a crass commercial move designed to target a black audience for hockey. It was believed that White brought more black fans to the game, and into MSG in particular, than ever before. The question of blaxploitation was an issue from the outset, even if the denials were as calculated as its affirmations. Writing in the *New York Times* (1 June 1972), reporter Gerald Eskenazi quotes Raiders GM Marvin Milkes to the effect that: "We very carefully tried to explain to Alton and his attorney that we weren't exploiting him … in fact, the fact that he was black was never even mentioned in the negotiations." Indeed, later in the story, Milkes adds that "it was unlikely that White's signing would create a large core of black hockey fans in New York." White alone, of course, could not be expected to create such a fan base, since he was, after all, the only black player in the WHA and NHL at the time, that is, one of 520 players. Indeed, he was realistic in his assessment of the situation, noting that high ticket prices would keep black fans out of the rink. The critical mass simply did not exist. White only played thirteen games in New York before he left for Los Angeles to finish the season with the Sharks. He played the following year with this team, and 1974-75 proved to be his last WHA season; the LA Sharks folded, and White was picked up by a short-lived squad called the Michigan Stags, a team which played part of the year as the Baltimore Blades. All told, he played in a total of 145 games.

Significantly, in 1972, the attitude of marketing, of identifying and exploiting markets through the creation of "products" designed for them, was not yet the natural attitude of professional hockey, even though the idea of gaining access to the urban black market in the US is now an accepted part of league strategies of expansion and arena location in major American cities. The media presentation of White was a sign of things to come.

The summer of 1972 in New York saw James Brown, Sly and the Family Stone, and Ike and Tina Turner funkify the MSG-owned Roosevelt Raceway on Long Island during the Festival of Hope. The Newport Jazz Festival featured a stunning lineup which included Sonny Stitt, Thelonious Monk, Sarah Vaughn, Dizzy Gillespie and others. Jean Dubuffet's *Group of Four Trees* was plopped down in front of the Chase Manhattan Bank. Ali pounded George Chuvalo in Vancouver. And White signed with the Raiders. The effect was soon felt as the Washington team iced two black players, Bill Riley and Mike Marson, in 1974. The importance of White cannot be found in his performance but, rather, in the fact that with his signing the colour barrier in pro hockey, which was broken but still very much intact, was successfully assaulted for a second time with more immediate and long-lasting effects. This

93

double breaking of the colour barrier in hockey is a good example of how a broken line can connect with other racist and reactionary attitudes, reasserting and reassembling itself in new, perhaps even more mutant strains.

94

ATHLETES AS PETS

In *Landscapes*

of Modern Sport, John Bale advances the provocative idea that "the sportscape or athlete to which we show affection is the athletic analogue of the garden or the pet."[1] Maple Leaf Gardens, he points out, doesn't contain any shrubs, but it nonetheless remains a garden, if only euphemistically, as a sportscape aestheticized through horticultural and architectural imagery. This garden is full of "pets" disciplined, functionalized, steroid-enhanced, and exhaustively trained to perform.[2] These athletic pets are dominated so that they may best receive the affection of the spectators, their owners, and even, in extreme cases, their parents. Hockey netminders often adopt animal motifs when having their masks painted: ex-Toronto Maple Leaf goaltender Felix Potvin is nicknamed "The Cat," for example. Like the use of animals in military contexts (in advertisements for weapons and equipment in professional magazines and the decoration of airplanes), a single attribute (stealth, strength, speed, agility) is abstracted from a given species, exaggerated, and reconnected with a new thing or activity. We should not, however, expect all animal motifs to be used positively. Distortions are commonplace; think of mascots whose imbecility is supposed to provide light entertainment between breaks in the action. But what is being played for its amusement value is the representation of an animal as a mentally and physically challenged child. This kind of mascot is in a direct genealogical line with cartoon characters whose flaws define their characters.

The training thesis has been in circulation in less developed forms for some time now. In his discussion of the ambiguous healthiness of sports in "Sports Chatter," from *Travels in Hyperreality*, Umberto Eco maintained that one of the "first degenerations of the contest" involves "the raising of human beings dedicated to competition. The athlete is already a being who has hypertrophied one organ, who turns his body into the seat of an exclusive source of continuous play. The athlete is a monster."[3] The dedication to "total instrumentalization" makes the athlete a monster or, better, to follow Bales, a pet. But pets, while often distorted through selective breeding and the aesthetic determinations of what features are desirable for a given species on the show circuit, are also dearly loved, especially when they perform for their caretakers. While Eco recognizes that the athlete is dedicated to sports training regimes, however brutal and unhealthy they may be, Bales elides the matter of dedication. There has never been a greyhound, to use other words, that was dedicated to being trained to over-race and starved. Many persons do, however, submit to exhaustive and repetitive training routines; whether these routines are fundamentally abusive is an important question.

96

By changing the register of the analogy ever so slightly, however, we are thrown back to the identification of black slaves as domesticated farm animals and slaveholders as wild predators, poignantly employed in the classic American slave narrative of Frederick Douglass, *Narrative of the Life of Frederick Douglass, An American Slave: Written By Himself* (orig. 1845). What this autobiographical narrative reveals is the prevailing nineteenth century image of the black slave as a healthy animal, who, if needs be, will be broken through labour, tortured and/or murdered, and selectively bred. It is not very far from the racism of the Old South to contemporary stereotyped representations of black athletes, that is, from animalization to the petishism of focusing the so-called naturally expressive black body. Indeed, consciousness, as we learned in the case of Canadian sprinter Ben Johnson after the debacle in Seoul, was denied to him insofar as he was figured as a "primitive," an animal-machine. Race and, indeed, gender oppression functions through animalization, as does economic exploitation.

Notes

1. John Bale, *Landscapes of Modern Sport*, London: Leicester University Press, 1994, p. 44.

2. "The fact is that professional players offer their labor power to the factories of spectacle in exchange for a wage. The price depends on performance, and the more they get paid the more they are expected to produce.

Trained to win or to win, squeezed to the last calorie, they're treated worse than racehorses. Racehorses? Paul Gascoigne likes to compare himself to a factory-raised chicken: controlled movements, rigid rules, set behaviors that must always be repeated," Eduardo Galeano, *Soccer in Sun and Shadow*, London: Verso, 1998, p. 205.

3. Umberto Eco, "Sports Chatter," in *Travels in Hyperreality*, San Diego: Harcourt Brace Jovanovich, 1986, p. 161.

DISCIPLINING ROAD HOCKEY

The town

of Gananoque in Eastern Ontario recently tightened up its By-Law No. 83-32 concerning the regulation of traffic and parking. In addition to what you might expect to find in a traffic by-law, there is the following sub-section on the matter of "Playing On Roadway Prohibited":

> 1. No person shall play or take part in any game or sport upon a roadway.

Sociologists of sport in Germany such as Lüder Bach, for instance, have shown a keen interest in the study of informal sports activities and facilities.[1] The informality of such sports means the absence of a wide variety of prerequisites: institutional, individual, organizational. The proliferation of informal sports occurs generally in the context of the absence of legal prohibition, which is only to say that the facilities being put to use allow for a secondary use above and beyond their primary uses. To put this more forcefully, primary uses are decoded for the sake of new practices which remake and remodel rules of participation. For generations of Canadian boys and girls, roadways have been places for playing road or "ball" hockey, skipping, hopscotch, or just throwing around any number of balls, frisbees, etc. Of course, quiet roads are preferred to busy routes but, no matter, since there is usually a safety protocol in effect: when a car appears its presence is announced ("Car!"), the action stops, equipment is moved, and then the game resumes. The smallest, weakest, and the least well-equipped often get to play, although there is no denying the effects of neighbourhood pecking/picking orders. Pick-up games of hockey are celebrated in mass cultural phenomena such as television advertisements for beer in which a game spontaneously breaks out in the financial district, bicycle stands are used for nets, a briefcase substitutes for a goaltender's stick, and the game is interrupted by the appearance of a streetcar. A parody of this Labatt's beer commercial on the satirical *This Hour Has 22 Minutes* comedy show, which substituted curling for hockey, underlined the commercial message: "anything can happen when you drink in the afternoon." To which the beer company has responded, echoing the precession of simulacra, with a curling commercial.

In effect, the Gananoque by-law makes road hockey a traffic offense, not to mention further eroding the rights of pedestrians. Moreover, it pushes informal street sports toward more formal frames, perhaps not all the way to the boarded iceless surface and the ball hockey association, but at least into parking lots and playgrounds, thereby displacing other activities. This legal reterritorialization of the roadway is designed to enable the cops to actually trap and deform the flows of unorganized sporting desire and its fuzzy, neighbourhood aggregates. The push is on towards organization and commercial interests: join the league, pay a fee, buy this equipment, consume! If you won't cooperate: pay a fine!

Notes

1. Lüder Bach, "Sports without Facilities: The Use of Urban Spaces by Informal Sports," *International Review for Sociology of Sport* 28 (1993): 281-96 and Brad Shore, "Marginal Play: Sport at the Borderlines of Time and Space," *International Review for Sociology of Sport* 29 (1993): 349-66.

DOWN AND OUT IN THE NHL

Deprivation has

reached a new low. Goaltenders are begging: in transit shelters and subway stations around Maple Leaf Gardens, as well as on television spots broadcast during games, not to mention in Nike's promotional booklets distributed in the Gardens to launch the campaign.

But these are not just any goalies. These are humiliated, down-and-out goalies reduced to scratching together a living by panhandling, cab driving, breakdancing, cycle messengering, janitorial work, yard work, and hot dog vending.

Sure, they've kept their equipment, thirty-odd pounds of rawhide, high-tech plastic, wire-enforced padding, clunky skates and heavy sticks. But times are tough for these guys because, after all, have you ever tried to peddle a bike or breakdance or drive a cab in full goalie gear? These goalies haven't learned to translate their skills, let alone change their equipment.

We are far, far away from Ken Danby's iconic goalie as a study in concentration, as well as from the anthropological noodling of the Hockey Hall of Fame, with its wall of "ritually" decorated goalie masks.

Why goalies? The advertising campaign is in support of a line of hockey skates promoted by fast skating and powerful shooting forwards, all in a sponsorship deal with Nike. In the campaign's narrative, the formidable skills of these forwards have resulted in the dismissal of a series of goalies from their respective teams. The collective story told by these goalies is printed awkwardly on torn pieces of cardboard, and held up for passersby to read: "I am a former NHL netminder. Please help. Read my story. Read my other goalie friends' stories. Read why you should never send either Mats Sundin, Jeremy Roenik, or Sergei Federov a birthday card."

Beaten goalies with dull skates and broken sticks have a hard time translating their netminding skills: "Will stop pucks for food," the sign of one reads; another offers private goaltending lessons and novel entertainment for parties. The insignias of their former teams represent an NHL merchandizing tie-in. Team logos are copyrighted property, after all. These goalies are licensed failures.

There are legions of homeless in New York and Toronto who are living evidence of the effects of Reaganomics and Ontario's current brand of economic and social Harrisment. There is supposed to be humour in the incongruity between the outfits and tasks performed by Nike's goalies. This humour is at the expense of the homeless, and, especially of the working poor. As manufacturing jobs leave the country, skills that were once employable become as useless as goalie equipment at a hot dog stand. The campaign implies that the fall from grace is a result of a personal shortcoming. No hint of structural matters here; neither a defenceman nor a right-wing ideologue in sight!

Tucked away in some of the images – on the hot dog wagon and the janitor's bucket – is the Nike logo. It isn't that the equipment of the working poor has a sponsor; rather, it is impossible to be independent, perhaps work at all, even panhandle, because everything is already owned by someone else and hence, they must have their fee. Despite itself Nike brings home the fact that we are living in the hell of a perpetual advertising event. Welcome to Nike Town, where even the soiled cardboard of the homeless bears a logo.

Nike's corporate luxury is to turn poverty and homelessness into an advertising icon, courtesy of its ad agencies, in the name of ice skates. No goalie I've ever seen could possibly stop a company like Nike when it is breaking full speed for the net. The market for hockey equipment is beginning to see some serious competition as footwear manufacturers get into the game.

This is the season of the goalie in advertising. Molson's, too, has its twelve-armed goalie monster in the "I Am Canadian" print campaign. Molson's goalie is not exactly the Hindu deity Krishna in a Maple Leafs uniform, as we have come to expect since the film *Masala* (directed by Srinivas Krishna) rearranged hockey theology, but more like Kali having a bad day. Like Nike, however, Molson's thinks of hockey in terms of a showdown: a forward in alone on a goalie. "Showdown" was a gimmicky individual skills competition developed in the late 1970s to keep hockey fans glued to the screen during breaks between periods, the heaviest times of advertising during broadcasts. Despite Molson's ad copy about the pursuit of goals not involving any "corporate boxes, five dollar hot dogs or million dollar scoreboards" – just the sort of things that a beer company with a vested interest in hockey actually aspires to – it's still just "me versus the monster." No team, no help, and the only one cheering if you beat the goalie is yourself. "I Am Canadian" is, in the advertising life, another way of saying that not even you are your own any more.

THE TEMPLE OF HOCKEY

The floor

plan of the Hockey Hall of Fame reveals a great deal about the metaphysics and ethics under-writing the current representations of the game. Essentially, the Hall sprawls along the east end of the concourse level of BCE Place, in the bowels of Toronto's financial district. It is an extension of the underground shopping concourse; in fact, the final stop on the official self-guided walk of the Hall (presented by John Armstrong in the Hockey Hall of Fame maga-zine) is a souvenir shop called the Spirit of Hockey. This shop cannot be avoided because it is also the Hall's exit. Commerce is the spirit of hockey, and its wares crystallize this spirit better, we are told, than "great memories" of the Hall and hockey itself.

The Hall presents one wave after another of history, internationalism, fragments of empire, family affairs, interactivity and video-induced passivity in the name of sponsorships: someone unfamiliar with the professional game might be fooled into thinking that this is a temple devoted to the *Toronto Sun*, Ford, Esso, Blockbuster Video, Speedy Muffler, Molson, TSN, Coca-Cola, etc. Commercial history is not only well provided for but intimately tied to the history of the game itself. Commercial ephemera originally tied to specific products – plastic buttons and instant desserts, coupons and gasoline, cards and bubble gum – become collectibles in heavily overcoded micro-markets but also serve as markers of historical phases (from the original six to expansion, the very idea representing the expansion of capital with the discovery of a wider American market and concomitant merchandizing opportunities like the interminable redesign of sweaters, the comic logos, etc.). Indeed, involvement in some aspect of the game can be demonstrated through souvenirs and, even better, through the ever-expanding universe of merchandise. The "family zone" figures the nuclear family as a consumption machine designed in the 1950s but built to last or at least accrue value as its own material history is translated into the obscure codes uttered by collectors in the throes of acquiring yet another piece of the puzzle. This vulgar capitalist ethics is but a warm-up to weightier justifications.

The hustle and bustle of the concourse gives way to the only part of the Hall at street level. The ascent to the Bell Great Hall is billed as the highlight of any visit. The Great Hall provides a direct line to the transcendental unity of hockey. It is the "core sanctuary of hockey's proud history" articulated by the presence of Lord Stanley's Cup, the focal point of the room, bathed in the kaleidoscopic light of the stained glass of the 45-foot high dome. This rococo sanctuary was the head office of the Bank of Montreal until 1949, and a branch until 1982, later rescued from disuse when the Hall opened in 1993. The bank vault is still in use, housing the original silver cup donated by Lord Stanley in 1893. Hockey and banking history bleed together in a glorious vision of nation and culture building. The Great Hall is a trophy room commemorating great hockey men (inducted members of the Hockey Hall of Fame), a male preserve to be sure, of the great white north. The architecture of banking still dominates the skyline of Toronto, just as it shaped the streetscape of the city in the nineteenth century. What would be more appropriate than an MBANX commercial featuring Stompin' Tom's 'The Hockey Song'? Here, the symbolic economy of hockey is obvious to everyone, even to so-called hockey purists sunk in their anti-labour meditations on the creation of the Lord. The Great Hall is described as a "quiet place in which to reflect on the richness of our past." Perhaps "the riches of the past" would have streamlined the message. It is a place of pilgrimage, with the cup itself playing the role of sacred relic. It is the sort of thing upon which one is compelled to lay hands. There are no annoying busy signals here. The connection is always clear as the cup soars toward the heavens, held aloft by the great heights of the city's towers of finance. Inspired by the French translation of Hockey Hall of Fame as *Le Temple de Renommée du Hockey*, I said a silent prayer for the Maple Leafs since only a God can save them now.[1]

104

Hockey and Culture

Notes

1. As I prepare this manuscript, the Buds are miraculously in first place. My prayer may have worked. Apologies are due to Martin Heidegger since I bastardized one of his famous later phrases; despite his impressive girth, Heidegger apparently liked to ski. Baudrillard once cancelled a visit to Toronto due to a knee injury resulting form a skiing mishap, an incident for which I was held responsible.

FURNITURE AND SPORT

The idea

that sport and furniture share something, beyond the commonplace of couch potatoes, wrapped in their armchairs, slowly baking before interminable sports broadcasts, does not immediately spring to mind. The unlikely terrain of the history of furniture design provides the sports enthusiast, as well as the connoisseur of stationary activity, not to mention those with a general interest in design, with a new machine for exercising their intellects. Notwithstanding that household furnishings both hard and soft are privileged places for the most satisfying of physical workouts, I want to draw attention to particular designs of chairs and tables that were inspired by other less private, but no less international, of pastimes. The challenge, then, is to think furniture together with sport. If "eat-sleep-sports" is your mantra, it may be best to respond to this challenge in your dreams.

Consider chairs. The Italian design group of Jonathan De Pas, Donato D'Urbino and Paolo Lomazzi, best known for their famous inflatable chair *Blow*, designed in 1970 a soft, leather-upholstered chair named *Joe* in the shape of a baseball glove. The name evoked the great New York Yankee slugger Joe DiMaggio, who was perhaps the first global sports star. For Italian audiences, DiMaggio was most importantly one of Marilyn Monroe's husbands; he was also the subject of a Simon and Garfunkel song, among other things. Like most baseball gloves which have the signature of a sponsor – a pro player – burnt into their palm, as well as a stitched-on manufacturer's label, this artifact of pop art sensibility was auto-graphed by the designers, and had the design group's label attached to it. In a similar vein in 1973, pop sculptor Claes Oldenburg executed a large baseball mitt in steel and lead, with a wooden ball, for an outdoor site in Greenwich, Connecticut. In the pop art domain the *Joe* chair was an unacknowledged precursor of Oldenburg's 12-foot high *Standing Mitt with Ball*, even though the steel sculpture was based on the glove worn by a first baseperson rather than that of a fielder.

Baseball was also the inspiration for Carmen Spera's wood-and-glass *Slugger* table of the early 1990s made for New York's Art et Industrie. The table has legs in the shape of baseball bats with weighted rings – the kind used for practice swings on the warm-up deck. The shape of the tapered bat, especially those that are fired to expose the grain of the wood, lends itself to the construction of tables, and perhaps even of pillar-like supports.

Canadian-born architect Frank Gehry is well known for his work as a furniture designer. His love of hockey and interest in the tradition of bentwood furniture – from the famous laminated plywood chair of Michael Thonet in the late nineteenth century, to the later modernist masterpieces of molded plywood built in the 1930s and 40s by Alvar Aalto, Marcel Breuer, and Charles and Ray Eames – dovetailed in the project he undertook for the Knoll Group of New York between 1989 and 1991. The chairs designed by Gehry were named after hockey terms: the side chairs, *High Sticking* and *Hat Trick*, and the arm chairs, *Power Play* and *Cross Check* (an armchair version of *Hat Trick* was also produced). They were woven out of wood strips, consisting of seven thin layers of maple laminated together; the ends of the long strips were then glued together. These were not nuts and bolts pieces, but curving and looping, soft-angled, and springy artworks resonant of reedwork and bushel baskets. Indeed, the curves of the arms and backs strongly suggest the curved blades of hockey sticks transformed into art furniture. For many young men, and more recently, young women as well, a traditional wood hockey stick, with a blade coated in fibreglass for strength, is a piece of bentwood with which they are intimately familiar, even though they may not know that the "lumber" they are carrying is likely cut from a species of tree native to Canada, White Ash.

Gehry's choice of names for his chairs are provocative: *High Sticking* and *Cross Check* denote infractions; *Power Play* and *Hat Trick* are, respectively, terms denoting the advantage enjoyed by a team when the opposing team has been assessed a penalty, and the scoring of three goals – in its purest form in a row – by a single player. The iconic resemblances suggested by these names between certain aspects of hockey and the design of the chairs themselves were in some ways more evident in the prototypes Gehry produced in his workshop than in the final versions, especially in the long vertical strips of the "high sticked" back, the "cross-weaving" of the seats of the armchairs, and his experiments with a triangular base. The chairs that went into production, however, were not restricted by resemblance but, rather, superseded it through the juxtaposition of diverse domains that not only required a certain amount of participatory completion by those who viewed and sat on them but also a sporting – that is a taking of risks – attitude toward the production of meaning. In fact, a good example of a stuffy commentary is found in the catalogue produced by the Montreal Museum of Decorative Arts in 1991 in conjunction with the exhibition of Gehry's *New Bentwood Furniture*. The matter of the origins of the names of the chairs is not even mentioned.

108   In a different cultural context and, by contrast to the lightness of Gehry's hockey chairs, Japanese designer Isamu Kenmochi's imposing *Kashiwado* chair of 1961 consisted of blocks of lacquered Japanese cedar, and was suitably named after a well-known sumo wrestler of the period.

The consideration of chairs and to a lesser extent tables enables me to meet the challenge of thinking furniture together with sport. This preliminary investigation of a relationship hitherto ignored provides an example of how the manifestations of sport as culture may be appreciated and, indeed, cultivated, beyond the commonplaces of blind followership demanded by the cult of masculine violence and the degradations of bourgeois spectacle with which sport is routinely and, reductively, saddled.

A BRIEF HISTORY OF THE DOG COLLAR

Is it

possible to write a history of the dog collar without writing a history of the domesticated dog? Yes, in principle, such a thing is possible because along the way the collar becomes detached from the animal and begins an intense circulation through the worlds of fashion, music, and popular culture. The question of how to formulate an answer reached a kind of fever pitch during my visit to Leeds Castle, near Maidstone in southern England, in which a most extraordinary show was on display: "Four Centuries of Dog Collars." Leeds Castle is greatly over-hyped and nowhere near Leeds; yet, one would be foolish to pass up an opportunity to see such a collection.

My visit was clouded by heady presuppositions. The absence of collared dogs in the history of modern art was, for me, an obstacle of sorts; I make this claim as a thinker of dogs in the context of the history of psychoanalysis, for instance, and in the study of the use of animals in advertising, what I like to call "pet technologies."[1] Sure, minor British painter Francis Barraud's *His Master's Voice* (1898-99) is an exception, notwithstanding the work's commercial fame as an advertisement, which had already begun by 1900, for the highest level of fidelity – not merely in the reproduction of sound and the mutual emotional attachments of dogs and their owners, but in the loyalty of consumers, especially with regard to the purchase of RCA recordings. None of the dogs of Modernist masters such as Gauguin,

Picasso, Mondrian, Marc, Klee, Miro, or Giacometti wear collars, although there is evidence of a keen interest in the flash and arc of leashes in Balla's futurist dachund, *Leash in Motion* (1912), and Bacon's menacing *Man with Dog* (1953). Pop and postmodernist dogs are rarely collared; Wegman's dogs in stuffed shirts are another matter altogether. They are *suits* in the most derogatory sense of the term. Still, collars can take on architectural significance, as in Dali's *Apparition of Face and Fruit Dish on a Beach* (1938), in which the dog embedded in the landscape sports as a collar a stone bridge decorated with three arches.

With the twentieth anniversary of the summer of hate recently behind us, one might think that the history of the present, at least as it concerns dog collars, was a matter for archivists of punk. After all, the metal-studded leather dog collar was a punk fashion statement equalled only by the safety pin. A catalogue of those who wore them, and how they displayed them, would be fascinating as a research document, but reveal little about the class struggles and incipient multiculturalism aimed at mainstream racism at the heart of the movement, even though a suburban Canadian kid might still wear a dog collar and act like a dog, even a Nazi Dog as one infamous Toronto punker called himself with an alarming air of commitment. The signification of dog and collar in punk culture could erase the progressive ideas of the movement by rather unambiguously invoking the German guard dogs that once patrolled the borders of Jewish ghettoes and thus serve as a sign of a fascist-racist politics. By a strange twist of semiotic fate, the collar might very well signify in some contexts under certain circumstances the struggle against racism in punk culture. The dog collar is a mobile signifier with no particular allegiances or frozen connotations.

As far as London goes, rather than shallowly signifying the halcyon days of King's Road fashion and pet shop fetishism of Westwood and McLaren, the dog collar reaches back into the nineteenth century of Victorian England and the street traders who sold dogs, brass collars, collection boxes and padlocks, on the Old Swan Pier and elsewhere. Dogs commonly carried padlocked collection boxes for charity fundraising. These collars were not destined for aristocratic hounds and the sporting life, but for the rigours of city life. The manufacture and sale of dog collars was a trade plied on special pitches around London. Leather collars were also popular during this period and there is one in the collection at Leeds with 7-cm spikes. Such collars date from at least Medieval times, however, and were employed in the hunting of wild game such as boars, bears and wolves. Indeed, fifteenth- to seventeenth-century iron collars manufactured in Germany and Austria featured broad plates linked by spiked rings or rows of spiked links without any backing. The emphasis was on protection rather than restraint. These contrast with the nineteenth century examples of engraved silver collars awarded at shows and coursing stakes to aristocratic hounds; still, silver presentation collars from Scotland (c. 1830) and England (c. 1838) themselves contrast with the white metal collars of late nineteenth century collection dogs working in the names of charities such as the Parade Committee.

I do not want to suggest that a history of the dog collar should confine itself to Continental Medieval and nineteenth century British examples. Anyone who takes on such a task would need to delve into the ornamentation of dogs (Anubis, the god of mummification, was sometimes represented as a dog) in ancient Egypt and in Greek and Roman cultures. Indeed, the connection I drew earlier between fascist punk culture and the collared dogs of National Socialism needs to be worked out against the background of Plato's comparison, in the *Republic* (2. 375a), of the attributes of the guardians of the state and watchdogs, both well-bred, unconquerable, lovers of wisdom. Perhaps all appropriations of the dog collar, despite its cultural mobility, must struggle against its ancient and mid-twentieth-century histories of reaction and racism in order to protect against these tendencies.

Notes

1. Pet technologies are communications and entertainment products marketed by association with certain attributes (actual, exaggerated and imagined) of dogs and other animals, primarily domesticates. For instance, AT&T's Call Minder telephone employed a watchdog; Sony's stabilizer system for CD players showed a dog with a CD in its mouth; a similar motif was used by Koss to promote its lifetime warranty on headphones, a policy which might very well save a friendship, when your best friend turns up with a well-chewed set of headphones in his mouth; and Nokia recently ran a campaign emphasizing man's new best friend, a cell phone. There are also cats, both wild and tame, evident in the mediascape, as well as other animals. GuardDog software is a recent example of the use of the collared dog as a pet technology for those who would like to keep their surfing private. The WatchDog page of TRUSTe, the non-profit privacy protection program on the web, sports a collared dog.

A PORTRAIT OF JESUS AS A YOUNG SCHWARZENEGGER

Imagine a

portrait of Jesus as a young Arnold Schwarzenegger and you have a pretty good idea about Stephen Moore's provocative book *God's Gym*.[1] It's not just the Son flexing in the weightroom, but the Father, too. And He's on steroids: "The wrath of God in the Bible is nothing other than 'roid rage," Moore speculates. This irascible, volatile God even began to grow breasts as the testosterone flooding the divine body produced by steroid use was met with the manufacture of estrogen. To make this claim about God's physical androgyny Moore stages a clever argument indeed; because the God of Israel only shows his/her back to Moses, s/he must be hiding something. Citing gym vernacular, Moore is straightforward about the divine muscle(wo)man's "bitch tits" or gynecomastia brought on by prolonged steroid use. Concomitantly, God's testicles may have shrunk, as Moore suggests, quoting the observation of a former Mr. Universe, to the size of "cocktail peanuts" (incidentally, this helps to explain the absence of crotch shots of Arnie and Lou Ferrigno in the *Pumping Iron* films). Moore adds of the Son, following John 2: 14-16, that Jesus was in throes of 'roid rage when he drove from the temple "all the sellers of iron-pumping paraphernalia (belts, straps, wraps), protein supplements, megavitamin packs, anabolic booster packs, posing trunks, posing oil, tan-in-a-bottle, muscle-shirts, muscle posters and muscle mags."

The equation is simple: "The Father bodybuilds ... and so Jesus too is a bodybuilder." Like father, like son, Moore quips. Jesus pumped iron, undergoing great suffering, a "murderous regime," it seems, not unlike his contemporary counterparts in Gold's Gym. Go(l)d's Gym in Venice, California, and Temple Gym, in Birmingham, UK, are sacred places in which one may find the extraordinary reigning Mr. Olympia, Dorian Yates, at the sight of whose body one observer is said to have gushed: "Oh, *Jesus!*" The other Jesus was often observed at the lesser temples of Galilee and Judea, and even enjoyed outdoor training, an activity promoted by Schwarzenegger himself for aesthetic reasons (natural tanning).

What a difference a set of brackets around a letter can make to an entire argument: Go(l)d's Gym. This sort of bracketing is a postmodern textual device *par excellence*, and it has the weight – no pun intended – usually afforded to an interjection, which isn't much. But it is, as Moore is well aware, a posing dais of its own, and it is often in brackets that he writes, registering our readerly gaze as we stand before a bodybuilding lecturer in New Testament studies showing us his autobiography. The soft, saggy academic body is not, for the most part, much to behold: pot bellies, hunched shoulders, flattened arses and pasty complexions are common enough. What a sight it is to behold the hypertrophied organs of iron-pumping lecturers!

113

Moore turns to Luke and John for evidence of Jesus' overtraining. The "three [days] on, one off" training regime of the modern gym was no equal to the seven-on system to which Jesus stuck most of his life; near the end of which, especially in the scene at the temple, he finally came around to a one-on, three-off routine: one day to blitz, and three to resurrect. "And what a workout it turns out to be!" Moore exclaims. When Jesus' spotters, Peter, James, and John fall asleep as he is warming up on the Mount of Olives, an angel descends and helps him through a gruelling session of squats, until Judas shows up and is staggered by Jesus' body. It is not until Jesus poses before Pilate that it is obvious that what floored the arresting party was Jesus' totally ripped body. Moore explains: "In bodybuilding parlance, the term 'ripped' and its synonyms … refer to the startling physical condition achieved by the contest-ready bodybuilder whereby he or she becomes a myological figure, a flayed man or woman, an ambulatory anatomy illustration." Moore employs examples from Medieval and Renaissance anatomy books containing drawings of flayed figures illustrating musculature to link these early muscle men with Jesus, whose crucified form sometimes served similar ends.[2]

And as everyone already knows, Jesus' back was totally ripped by the scourge wielded by the Roman soldier at the behest of Pilate. The main event at Golgotha was a letdown. It is obvious for Moore that Jesus peaked too soon; indeed, Jesus begins to "hold water" thereby blurring his musculature, a condition dreaded by bodybuilders. As we know, some nutter in the audience speared Jesus in the side; strange how this happens even today, as tennis star Monica Seles will attest. But the connection between Jesus and tennis is not accidental if one recalls that Baudrillard, in his well-known postmodern travelogue *America*, was astonished to find that in Salt Lake City "all the Christs are copied from Thorwaldsen's and look like Bjorn Borg." It is incredible to think that after only three days off, Jesus was back again and bigger than ever – bigger than even John Lennon could have imagined; Moore says he is "Brobdingnagian in bulk." Before the Supreme Judge, the risen Jesus takes the Mr. Universe title hands down.

The strange confluence of postmodernism, religion and sport has in the form of *God's Gym* produced a caricature so finely detailed and with such wonderful buoyancy that one can't help but wonder what it was that the author exaggerated in the first place. Oh – scholarship, that humourless, uncreative and stodgy pastime. The tabloidization of academic writing was pioneered by the cultural studies list at Routledge. *God's Gym* is a fine example of what happens when an academic goes tabloid: cultural gives to biblical studies a stage upon which to pose and flex.

The sociological question raised by *God's Gym* is whether or not weightlifting culture will be destroyed by being "discovered" by the academy and trendy professors eager for reproducible proof of their street cred. J.G. Ballard once exclaimed "leave us alone!" as the professors, full of themselves and some hastily digested theory, found their second wind in science fiction studies, and invaded the subculture with a vengeance. Borderline bodies have been all the rage for several years now, and the hypermasculine bodies of weightlifters are simply the latest to be pushed through the prevailing critical categories. Talk about being totally ripped (off).

Notes

1. Stephen Moore, *God's Gym*, New York: Routledge, 1996. Although Moore does not mention it, *Rocky* begins with a brutal boxing match under the watchful eye of a portrait of Jesus in a makeshift club called Resurrection A.C. The bodybuilding-warrior connection is, however, noted by Moore with reference to Stallone in particular.

2. In my review of Winnipeg-based artist Tom Lovatt's spring 1998 show at the Winnipeg Art Gallery, "The Human Position," I draw on Moore's book as a way to situate his totally ripped Christs, although Moore has little to contribute to Lovatt's use of the athletic male body to flag the intersections of contemporary notions of masculinity and homoerotic desire. Lovatt's Christs often wear cut-off jean shorts and appear to use the cross as a posing dais ("Refrains of Masculine Experience," *Border Crossings 17/2* [May 1998]: 52-3).

CONFESSIONS OF CARD COLLECTOR

I am

a collector. This is my confession. This thing, this compulsion, is in my family and probably goes back generations if anyone cared to trace it. The collecting gene has not been isolated. It's probably only a matter of time. How did I get started, you may be wondering? Without blaming anyone in particular, it was like this: I was young and, well, it was the gum, the gum that came with the cards. That pink plank, delicately dusted with an unidentifiable white substance with, now that I think of it, the odour of a manufactured object a little too real, a little more gummy than ordinary gum; sometimes, in the winter, the gum would freeze, or at least take on an appearance I imagined as frozen, and shatter like glass when separated from the waxy paper to which it tenaciously clung. Indeed, this gum was at the best of times a bit on the brittle side and hard to chew, but it was a constant in a hit-and-miss game of buying sports cards in search of the players I needed to complete my collection or build up my trade-able and disposable cards. It was easier to share the gum than the cards and it served to defuse more than few of the competitive flare-ups which were inevitable whenever I opened my packs of cards together with a fellow collector who happened to be searching for the same card, filled with the same hope and anticipation and ready to get physical about it. Children are, especially in the throes of collecting, cruel.

For me, the gum was not collectible, although I don't doubt that gum collectors found it fascinating. It was, after all, a strange substance and in every way inferior to most other kinds of gum. And it had a peculiar biomorphic character, something of the interior of the body in its colouration that simultaneously attracted and repulsed me, and I considered it a duty, the first duty of the collector, in fact, to eat it. This was my cannibal phase. It came with the territory. Which is only to suggest that I never understood those who threw the gum away in disgust. Of course it was disgusting. It was stale, poor quality gum with cavity-causing power. I have the teeth to prove it. The gum was not a sideshow; these were bubblegum cards. It was not an added-extra as if sports needed any more allure. It was the natural milieu of a young collector, an ecological niche of sorts in an unstable world. You have to understand: I had to eat that gum because it threatened the safety of my collection, it caused anxiety because it was a diversion that kept me from the safe haven of the cards themselves. I had to get it out of the way as quickly as possible so I could disappear into my collection and stop time. Cards were my pastime, literally, past time in a steady state that I could replay at will by running through the pieces once more, performed to the rhythm of a big pink wad of gum: smack, smack, smack.

117

So, as a boy, I collected sports cards. The first rule of collecting is that every piece only refers back to the collector. The cards exalted me. They were mine; it was my collection. They had value because I collected them; I made them precious. I can't emphasize this too much: the cards glowed in my possession and even the most common ones that nobody wanted had a preciousness that came from my singularity as a collector. Ultimately, the meaning of a card, as a collectible piece, is the collector.

The second rule of collecting is that the thing collected cannot have any practical use. If it once had one, it must be abstracted from its original context of use and become a piece in a collection. Cardboard cards of hockey, baseball and football players are totally useless and smell of bad gum. They are not even heavy enough to be used to clatter in the spokes of bicycles. These are virtues. The possession of a piece is at once satisfying and frustrating. But mostly the former. Security and sovereignty: these are the things a collection offers. Sure, collecting the whole set is a frustrating experience because there are pieces over which one has no control, and one desperately needs them, and has to leave the safety of the collection and get into messy negotiations in order to find them.

The idea that collecting is a compensation for active genital sexuality and is more intensely pursued during the latency period of seven to twelve years of age is a psychoanalytic explanation that rests on a dubious developmental theory (oral-anal-genital). My propensity for collecting was so well known that even girls took notice of it and volunteered to help me out. One neighbour in particular helped me immensely through the best offices of her older brother and provided me free of charge with speciality cards from the local gas station. I remember her fondly to this day and see her name occasionally on the titles of books she has authored. Collecting made me attractive, even as a curiosity. I was less interesting after my collecting years and it was only then that I really needed some anal occupation as a compensation. So, I held fast to my lifetime goal of becoming a bachelor and moving to San Francisco.

In my heyday I ruled a vast empire of cards. The home-made boxes in which I stored them were painted my favourite colours (orange and black, the colours of the SF Giants) and had sliding drawers with gold metal handles. I had many of these proto-filing cabinets. I was in training for a profession, or perhaps a position as a lowly office clerk; I didn't care. My domain was well-organized and I knew the whereabouts of all my pieces. I established yearly profiles and sets, as well as unique sub-sets such as the cards of aboriginal and black players in the NHL. Among my prize possessions I counted the 1953-54 Fred Sasakamoose rookie card; a defenceman on the ersatz tribe of Chicago, the Black Hawks, the description of whom included the racist nickname "Big Chief"; the 1963 Jim Neilson rookie card that didn't fail to mention he was "part-Indian"; and my coveted Willie O'Ree "Beehive," a black and white photo of him in his Boston uniform. They have served me well over the years and sustained my interest in the social and political aspects of the sportscape. I can't account for how I came to these interests. I had other more obscure passions for what surely counted as marginalia at the time and cultivated a keen sense of their attractiveness for they provided me with a singular measure that was irreducible to the collection proper, the yearly set of cards which could be dutifully checked off a checklist provided by the manufacturer. This meant that I might never have to face the crisis of a completed collection. Moreover, such value could not be in any way reduced to a price in the micro-economy of the greater collecting arena. While everyone was fighting over Bobby Hull and Gordie Howe, I could wallow in my symbolic sub-economies and esoteric pursuits, stalking the margins for the next minoritarian element that might appear at any moment in some hitherto unnoticed randomly distributed characteristics: players who wore headbands; players who were born in a faraway place called Saskatchewan.

And then my collecting ended, just like that. The collections themselves began to break apart – like my voice – and gather dust, and get lost in the shuffle until they were nowhere to be found. Luckily, a few pieces survived seemingly of their own accord. I am not ready to rebuild, though I found myself on the phone the other day talking to card shop wondering if they had in their possession a team photo from the mid-seventies of the LA Sharks including Alton White, but this was obviously an effect of this manuscript, wasn't it? Still, cards remain very good to think.

Followership can

be quite banal when it rises no higher than fandom. Cheering for only one team is a quick and easy way to acquire an unchanging identity and has very little to do with creativity, but much to do with the illusion of protection provided by like-minded persons and the static existence that comes from a narrowly focused allegiance. Fandom is unproductive, although this may be misunderstood because it seems to fly in the face of logo merchandizing and the mountains of swag available for marking one's territory. The display of team logos may be used to create and temporarily occupy territories, a particular section of a stadium, for instance, and may be supplemented with sonorous elements such as chants and songs, but by and large these presuppose territorial possession and allegiance (home turf) tied to aggression (and other specific goals like the satisfaction of hunger) rather than a form of art tied to expression, the creation and development of a style, and the very construction of a territory. Displaying your team's colours is a way to inherit a readymade territory rather than build one. Fandom is a comforting form of interaction that finds satisfaction in repetition and familiarity: Go Leafs Go is a refrain shouted by a crowd as it gathers itself together. In some sports such as soccer, the violence of followers is legendary.

Underneath the blaring rock music of nondescript stadia, tasteless food, boring games, faceless expansion teams, someone up in the nosebleed seats has freed himself or herself from the impulse to dominate the other team and merge into a mass, a sea of coordinated, trademarked colours and patterns, and is scribbling away at something on a hot dog napkin that will develop into the libretto of a revolutionary opera, *The Orioles in Cuba*, perhaps. This is not that romantic figure, the genius who works alone, because rhythms are established between fellow librettists scattered here and there in different territories making their contributions, and melodies are collaborated upon by assorted artists – chorus masters and composers – on the same piece in the same place. When a crack opens in a territory that has been loosened from aggression, when the US opens to Castro through baseball rather than trade, improvisation becomes possible. The territory opens at a point that no one could have predicted. A crack, yes, but nine innings worth! No indeterminate opening to worry about here. This was a sober operation coded by the baseball rulebook and watched over by umpires. Baseball: the only enduring American metaphysics. And this is a solution to the impasse of followership: a break in a tired refrain.

This condition shifts one's focus onto apparatuses of capture, the most common of which across several media are slow motion and instant replay. Running time, for instance, refers to the length of a film measured in minutes. But running time is also the time accorded to running in its commonplace cinematic representation through slow motion. Running is captured in slow motion and transformed into a luxurious meditation on movement rendered viscous. This is a privileged kind of heightened perception varying in relation to the dominant speed-motion of the rest of the action in the film. It is the privileged means of inspection and apprehension of running in its most fluid form; slow motion saturates running. By contrast, the instant replay is a staple of video and television and has none of the charm of slow motion; but it may reveal something remarkable like the snapshots of Muybridge's galloping horses. True, the unanalyzed replay is visual fast food. It becomes a domain of analysis when it is played in slow and stop motion and presents the opportunity for expert and colour commentary of the sort pioneered in hockey by Howie Meeker and in football by John Madden. It is, then, a kind of moving blackboard open to the analysis of otherwise indecipherable patterns and flows. The slow-motion replay is as valuable to coaches and analysts as it is to officials. Today, it alone allows for the putatively fair application of the rules when perception fails for whatever reason, having been overcome by speed, for example. This application is considered problematic precisely because it is abstracted from the movement of the event at issue: in attempting to make an episode reveal itself, one reverts to photographic method or a series of stills to which movement and mobility are then added. This use of the replay tries to reconstitute movement from a series of snapshots which are only partially reunited into a whole: the choice of immobile images – the relations between some of which will be considered relevant to the call – makes this a highly selective and unfair process for many. Consider, for example, the abuse through overcoding of slow motion by the defenders of the LAPD in the Rodney King case: slow motion in this case turned clear evidence of police brutality into an argument that King was attacking the police!

Statistics such as averages and percentages, as well as summaries and related overviews, often in forms peculiar to each sport, also attempt to capture sporting events. This form of capture by means of quantitative reduction is a simulation model without any purchase on sports. It is, however, a completely coherent and transparent method of representation. It is a favourite of the print media and those who have nothing more to say about a game other than the three or four words that fit in between the high and low score, from which so much sports-related comedy is derived.

One is always following behind a team or a sport because it is impossible to keep abreast of either of them. The sporting phylum is remarkably rich in singularities from which may be deduced and assembled constellations staggering in their complexity. It is a question of keeping up and running behind, even if this takes a creative turn. The flows are too rich and detailed to do otherwise. This book, which considers these flows in cultural and political terms, is also caught in a catch-up game of new events, late-breaking results, and fresh references. Despite the efforts of fandom, collecting, statistics, slow-mo and instant replay, we cannot capture sport. Sport captures us.

COLOPHON

Colophons – notes that explain the design, typesetting, and printing of a book – are becoming increasingly rare in modern publishing. We feel that all parts of the process of producing a book have political implications, and include these short paragraphs as a declaration of our pride in and responsibility for our work as designers, typesetters, and publishers. As well, a colophon can provide a rare view of the usually unseen, but often fascinating, world of book production.

Contest is set in Caslon, a contemporary version of the typeface first designed by William Caslon in 1722. We have chosen it because of its classic, open appearance, which makes it an elegant and readable typeface. These qualities are no doubt responsible for Caslon's enduring popularity; it has been in wide use since being adopted by English printers in the early eighteenth century, when it replaced the primarily Dutch typefaces that had long predominated. Caslon is most often criticised for its italics, which are considered unnecessarily florid.

The main text is set in 11-point type on a 13-point line. The notes are set in 9-point type on a 13-point line. Chapter titles are set in Futura T, 12-point type on a 14.4-point line.

All layout and design was done in-house on a Power Macintosh G3/233 and a Power Macintosh 6500/250, using PageMaker 6.5 and Photoshop 5.

The book was printed and bound by the workers at Harpell Printing of Ottawa, Ontario on 50lb. #2 offset paper.